BUILDING COMMUNITY

A memoir and
conversation starter

Sandra j. Combs
Author/Publisher

Building Community
A memoir and conversation starter

ISBN 978-1-7328498-0-8 (softcover)

This book is dedicated to everyone named within. Thank you for being part of my community.

And especially to KJ and Gracie, of whom I am very proud.

CONTENTS

Introduction

The intent of this book is simple. I believe that one of the best tools I have at my disposal to build community or a sense of community with those around me is the sharing of my stories. When I share a story with someone else, I am trusting the listener or reader by giving that person a glimpse into my life. Similarly, when someone is telling me a story, I connect with that person through the exchange of ideas and often shared experiences. I am a storyteller at heart. While that is my passion, it may not be yours. We all have tools and talents at our disposal that allow us to connect with others in meaningful ways. This book explores that premise and encourages dialogue about other ways we can engage in community building. I share my ideas by using stories from my own life and about people who are part of my community. My experiences are my own. I invite you to take my stories and use them as a catalyst for reflecting on ways you build community with those around you.

The first two stories I am going to share are about how this all began and how this book developed.

Building Community with Our Stories

In October 2016, I began participating in a local open mic storytelling event. If you are familiar with The Moth (check out themoth.org) this event is set up in that same format. The monthly hosts are Bryan and Shelly. Bryan is an incredible storyteller. He is personable, friendly, and is the kind of guy you wish was your big brother. When he tells a story, you feel as if you were there when it happened. Shelly is a different sort … and I mean that with great respect. She too is a talented storyteller. Shelly is artsy and a great supporter of the local music scene. She has a rough edge about her and in 2017 had many challenges – physically, financially, emotionally. When she tells a story, you want to go up and give her a big hug afterwards. Or, take her to a corner shop and just chat over a Kahlua and coffee as indie music plays in the background. In part, I credit these two for planting in my mind the genesis for this book.

The local storytelling events are in one sense competitive. Teams of judges are selected from the audience and can give storytellers a score up to 10 points. In the 18 times that I have taken to the microphone locally, I have finished in second place more times than not. I have also competed in Louisville and Detroit, placing third in Michigan. I have told my friends that I am quickly developing a Susan Lucci complex. Ha! The rules for this form of storytelling are simple: the stories must be told first person with no notes, they must be true, and they must be between five and six minutes long. Shelly is the time keeper and often uses a set of small meditation balls which when shaken at the five-minute mark give off a subtle chime noise. The balls are blue and belong to her husband, and yes, she uses a related joke every month.

On many occasions Shelly tells the audience that while scores are kept, the real purpose for the evening is not about who wins or loses. Shelly reminds us that the main purpose is to build community through our stories. Bryan has said that the stage is not a court or a field. It is more like a library where stories are free for the taking. While I really, really want to win these competitions, I have come to understand that Shelly and Bryan are correct.

What makes this monthly event one of the coolest things in which I participate is the fact that the storytellers are all unique. Each month a topic is announced. That's the other rule I failed to mention – stories must be related to the evening's topic. Because the storytellers come from different backgrounds, their stories take the audience down different paths. On stage, storytellers have told of near-death experiences, emotional or sexual abuse, and some of the most hilarious moments of their lives – and everything in between. Some of us are regulars, but each month newbies step up and participate. Storytellers are introduced and often when they begin to speak all we know is that person's name. By the time the storyteller exits stage left, we have seen a bit of his or her life unfold in the span of six minutes. And suddenly – boom – that person is now a member of our storytelling community.

In my experience, the real community building happens not when I step on the stage, but when I step off. This has led me to rethink what I understand about vulnerability and the part it plays in connecting with others.

In 2015 and 2016, I was in bi-weekly counseling as my second marriage was coming to an end. After my first divorce, I made the mistake of burying my emotions and not addressing them. That came back to bite me in the butt several years later. This time, I didn't want to make that same mistake; and, quite frankly, I needed help in understanding why I had two failed marriages. One day my counselor, Barbara, asked me what would happen if I allowed myself to be vulnerable, rather than having to be in control all the time. I remember shuddering and replying, "Why on earth would I want to do that?" I wasn't questioning my need to back off having to control so many things. I simply didn't like the word "vulnerable," feeling it implied weakness. Getting up on stage and sharing stories about my life, and doing the same in this book, doesn't feel weak to me. Quite the contrary. It has been empowering and has allowed me to engage others in ways I never previously understood. I have come to recognize that vulnerability is a key element in connecting with others. If you want to learn more about this, check out books and videos by Brenè Brown. She is an engaging expert on the topic of vulnerability.

The more I tell my stories, the more I have come to realize the impact those stories have on others. You'll read more about that in Chapter 3. This led me to consider other ways we can impact those around us and how we can build community with others.

So, that's where the initial idea for this book began. The outline for the book came together in the wee hours of a winter morning on January 9, 2018.

A Blast of Inspiration

I am 53 years old. If you happen to be within this general age range, perhaps you have experienced nights when you wake up at 2:30 a.m. with your mind racing and your body restless. Most of my friends tell me they do the same, except those who use a CPAP machine. Apparently, that is a miracle invention.

On that January night I woke up and started journaling and before I knew it an hour later I had my chapters outlined. The thoughts came rapidly and abundantly. I couldn't write quickly enough. It was as if the ideas that had been bouncing around in my head for over a year all came together at one time. I put the pen and paper down, turned off the light and said a short "thank you" prayer for the inspiration. Then more thoughts came to mind, so I flipped the light back on and wrote a draft of Chapter 7. Pen down, light off. More thoughts. Light on, pen to paper and more writing. Pen down, light off. Then I had the idea that I had better write about that early morning experience. Light on, pen to paper. It was at this point that I began to chuckle, hoping my neighbors weren't confusing the flickering light for some sort of coded distress signal.

The next morning, I was simultaneously exhausted and energized. Four days later, over a long, snowy three-day weekend which included recognition of Martin Luther King, Jr., I ended up writing about 30,000 words in 65 hours, minus time needed for eating and sleeping. I trusted my outline and the inspiration I had been given, didn't worry about editing, and just let the stories flow. On several occasions I had to get up from my computer and walk away, especially when writing the *Spreading Sonshine* and *Serenity* chapters. To say this was the most intense, creative weekend I have ever had would be a gross understatement. The words and stories poured out as if I had been storing them in a pressure cooker that suddenly began to steam.

With that, what is to come is a creation I share with you wrapped around the notion of building community. Each chapter discusses on one way we can connect with others. I state the focus for the chapter and offer a single trait under the chapter title which I believe is essential to connecting with others. I offer stories as discussion starters. And then, at the end of each chapter, I ask questions to spark conversation or reflection about your own experiences. I have also included scripture references for those who will find that meaningful.

In writing my stories, I recognize that this book may come across as allowing you to peek into my diary or to read my memoir. I am entrusting parts of my life story to you. This goes back to my understanding of being vulnerable. Know that the intent goes well beyond simply telling my own stories, although you can skip the discussion elements and read the book that way. My goal is to inspire others to find meaningful ways to connect, building positive community along the way.

~ ~ ~

Focus of Chapter 1:

Social Media is one tool at our disposal to build a sense of community with others. I offer an example of someone I know who does this extremely well as a means of starting a conversation on how we can use this tool better.

~ ~ ~

Chapter 1: One Post at a Time

Intentional

It may seem odd for me to start a book on building community with a chapter on social media. Too often social media becomes divisive, with political posts or rants against this person or that store or some movement. When sitting in front of a screen it is easy to forget that real people are reading our posts. I contend that we are all either building community through social media or bashing community. I have yet to come up with anything in between. This is not to say that people shouldn't express their opinions; to the contrary. My encouragement here is to do so with an attitude of building community and engaging dialogue. One dear friend of mine who is great at building community online is Myrna. To explain my relationship to Myrna I need to tell you about her parents.

Meet Lewis and Frances

When I was in high school, I attended a local United Methodist Church in Broken Bow, Oklahoma. Lewis and Frances were youth leaders and over the years adopted me as one of their own children, in every sense of the word except no judge was involved and no court order existed. While Frances passed away several years ago after a hard-fought battle against ovarian cancer, Lewis only recently passed away in early 2018. I was scheduled to go visit Lewis over Martin Luther King, Jr. weekend, the same weekend I ended up writing the first draft of this book. I knew he was aging and ailing and I had been told I should go before early signs of dementia increased. On December 28 I got a call from Myrna telling me I didn't have time to wait for the holiday weekend. Lewis' health had declined rapidly, so I hopped a plane on New Year's Eve and flew to Dallas. When the second leg of my flight was cancelled, I hurried to the rental car area and drove three hours to the hospital.

Sometimes when people are in the final stages of life, they decline, have one or two rebound days, and then begin their final descent to death. That Sunday, Lewis was on the second of his rebound days. I entered the room and he recognized me, reached for my hand, and said it was good to see me. Myrna and her brother, Bob, had been tag teaming 24/7 so someone was always with Lewis. They graciously allowed me to stay with him for the next 9 hours while they took a much-needed break. I was present on Monday as well, along with a hired caregiver (Althe, a true angel on earth), but Lewis was non-responsive that day. I will share with you here the email I sent to Myrna the following weekend, two days after being told that Lewis had passed away.

Myrna (and Bob), I have tried for several days to explain to my local support system just how humbled I was to make the trip to Texarkana last weekend and see Lewis. I am in awe of God's timing, allowing me to be there on a day when Lewis was alert and cognizant of my presence. I was so honored that you allowed me to stay with Lewis while you both took a much-needed break, if even for a few short hours.

As I sat in his hospital room, quietly in his presence, my emotions were all over the board. (Something I know you can relate to recently.) Every so often he would stir, and I was afforded short spurts of time to speak with him. I told Lewis, straight out, that he and Frances have been the two most influential people in my life. I would be nothing without the love and support that they showed me over the years. Lewis thanked me for saying that, as he slipped back into rest. Later I asked him if he remembered this event or that event, to which he responded, "I remember that well."

Around 7:30, the evening nurse, Alli, came to assess Lewis as she began her shift. First, she wanted to determine his mental status. She asked him, "Do you know what year this is?" "Yes, I know that," he responded. "It's '18." Alli and I chuckled, figuring that was close enough given that it was New Year's Eve. She next asked him if he knew who the president of the US was. "Yes, yes, I know that too," Lewis said. "It's ... pause ... Troupe. Ronald Troupe." Again, close enough.

After asking these questions, Alli wanted to physically examine Lewis. At one point she said, "Mr. Stiles, I need to lift up your gown for just a moment." Without missing a beat, Lewis said, "Ok, but I'll tell you now, you're not going to find anything you can use under there." (Dementia has a way of removing filters.) *I almost fell out of my chair laughing. Alli, in return, kept her composure and professionalism and simply said "Well, since all I need to do is check your chest pump we'll be just fine."*

Other than these moments of both awareness and humor, I simply sat quietly in that room. I found myself looking at the walls, reading the posters, trying to take in every aspect of that experience. I found myself reflecting over the times when Lewis and Frances parented me and loved me for who I was/am. Years of love and support came flooding back. And I treasured every moment. I am forever grateful to them and to you.

I have intentionally isolated myself this weekend, after hearing of Lewis' passing. For the most part, I have stayed home, just listening to my heart. In that process, I know what a rare gift I was given last weekend, to be there at exactly the right time and to have the opportunity to once again reiterate my love for your parents.

With that, I am not going to come to Oklahoma for the funeral. I know that you will be surrounded by family, the community and the church and that they will lift you up in your sorrow and celebrate with you the legacy that Lewis has left behind. Myrna, that was a beautiful tribute you posted on Facebook. And the loving responses are already pouring in. I trust you both will find comfort in the words others share.

For now, know that even if I am not physically present on Friday, I am there in spirit and in love. And I will be cherishing every memory that I have been gifted, dating back many, many years. My heart is full of love and peace. Last weekend was the most important trip. It afforded me closure and that was a most precious gift. I will be in touch. With much love, respect and gratitude ...

How to Use Social Media Well

When I became close to Lewis and Frances, Myrna was away in college. She is five years older than me. Over the years I was closer to her sister Mary Lee. The last time I saw Myrna prior to my visit to see Lewis in the hospital was at Mary Lee's funeral after she died from her own hard-fought battle with colon cancer.

In late 2016, Myrna began selling a line of hair products. She was retired and looking for not only new income but the answer to some thinning hair issues of her own. She reached out to me and asked if I would like to hear her pitch. I listened and, wanting to support her, agreed to purchase some products. We then became friends on Facebook.

Myrna is phenomenal in using social media to build her business. She posts thought-provoking questions, simply to engage others in dialogue. She asks things like, "What is your biggest source of stress right now?" or "What is one thing you are grateful for today?" or "What did you do today that was for you and you alone?" She posts shout-outs to her sales team when individuals reach certain goals. She promotes flash sales and the top 10 reasons why the products she sells are of value. She often live streams short messages of inspiration. I will admit that I am in awe of this point. I can barely turn my "smart" phone off and on much less know how to live stream something.

Myrna wrote a book in 2017 and used social media to promote it. She also engaged family and friends in the process, posting two pictures she was considering for her author's photo, asking for feedback.

As Myrna traveled with her husband Dan for a planned month-long visit with her father over the holidays, she used social media to keep family and friends informed as Lewis' health declined. But more than that, she freely offered followers a glimpse into her own emotions, posting, "Today is hard" or "I'm tired." She shared pictures of Lewis, from the time he was a young boy on the family's farm to recent family gatherings. As she took trips down memory lane, we went with her. Others shared their own memories, creating a community of people tied by bloodlines or friendship and shared grief over losing Lewis.

Through social media I have watched Myrna build her business, inspire others, and share her grief. I see pictures of quilts that she has created. I see photos of trips to Nicaragua where Myrna is involved in humanitarian mission work. I see pictures of her son, a former Marine, as many thank him for his service. I see her daughter who has blossomed into a lovely young woman. I am tied to Myrna because of Lewis and Frances, but I am better connected to her because of social media.

Myrna is a very genuine, unassuming person. She is inspiring in that she helps build community through a true passion for helping others, encouraging people to dialogue, and by being willing to open herself up to others. And she does this, in part, through social media.

Build, Don't Bash

Social media provides momentary respites from our daily lives. I appreciate the posts from a friend of her winter vacation to Puerto Vallarta as I stand looking out at the six inches of snow which fell on my backyard overnight. Social media affords opportunities for investigating shared interests. I have friends who are "foodies" and love to cook. We swap recipes and pictures of our meals. Social media offers the opportunity for local bands trying to build a following. I always make a point of commenting on their page when I attend one of their shows to aid their efforts.

On the other hand, there are some people I don't follow on social media. I have one friend that I refuse to follow on Facebook because we are such good friends otherwise. There is little if anything that she does not know about me. I think the same is true in reverse. We don't need Facebook or social media to stay connected. Those are by far the best relationships of all.

In 2017 and 2018, the most divisive posts that I have seen on social media have been on hot button topics such as politics or gun control. We are moved as a nation by the horrors of deaths in our schools. We are frustrated with bipartisan efforts to thwart progress in lieu of real change in many areas. People are calling others out because of their beliefs, rather than engaging in meaningful, intentional dialogue about ways to find common ground. This is where I truly believe what I said earlier – we are all either building community with our words or bashing the other side. Wherever dialogue happens, it is important to be intentional about our purpose and our words. Facebook and other platforms are powerful tools for the expression of beliefs. They are also powerful tools for the separation of community. But utilized correctly, Facebook or other social media platforms can offer initial blocks on which communities are built and nurtured … one post at a time.

PS: On the night that Lewis died, January 5, Myrna's husband called and left me the message that Lewis had passed. Later, when I retrieved the voicemail, I called Myrna back to talk to her. At the end of that conversation, she said to me out of the blue, "I don't know why, but I have been thinking that I need to tell you to write a book." We had never discussed this before. Her comment was totally unexpected. But four days later, in the wee hours of the morning, that off-handed comment began to take shape.

Chapter 1 Reflection

"Love suffers long and is kind; love does not envy; love does not parade itself, is not puffed up; does not behave rudely, does not seek its own, is not provoked, thinks no evil; does not rejoice in iniquity, but rejoices in the truth; bears all things, hopes all things, endures all things."
1 Corinthians 13:4-7

Q1: Look back over the pages of Chapter 1. What words or sentences did you underline? What parts of the story of Lewis and Frances or of Myrna resonated with you?

Q2: What types of social media do you use? Think of a time that you have found yourself "unfriending" or unfollowing someone? Why did you feel the need to do that?

Q3: Who do you follow on social media that makes you smile when you see their posts? Who do you follow that inspires you? How does that person inspire you?

Q4: If you were to take the scripture from 1 Corinthians and use that as a measuring stick for your own social media activity, how would you fare? Would others see you as rude or boasting, or would they find words of truth, hope and love in your posts?

Space intentionally left blank for your own thoughts.

Space intentionally left blank for your own thoughts.

~ ~ ~

Focus of Chapter 2:

Hospitality is one of my strongest gifts. I love to entertain family and friends. There have been times when I have been hesitant to do so because I compared what I have to what others have. As you read, consider what your strongest gifts are in relation to building community and how comparisons can hinder that connection.

~ ~ ~

Chapter 2: Welcome to My Home

Hospitable

One of my favorite things to do is entertain in my home. Rephrase – my ABSOLUTE FAVORITE thing to do is entertain in my home. I love the feeling of extending hospitality to my friends and family, knowing that this is a great way to build community.

At the time of writing this book, I had lived in my rental home for just over three months. I owned my previous home for 16 years. I loved that home which was the setting for so many memories. I bought it when my children were five and three; they are now in their 20s. Holidays, birthdays, weekend sleepovers, the Super Bowl … special days or ordinary days offered opportunities for me to entertain. And I took advantage of them all.

I am a planner and entertaining lends itself well to planning. I pick a theme around which I will plan a menu, often write an invitation, decorate. I love entertaining on a patio, although that is hard to do the first Sunday in February. Early on, I was a little intimidated by the thought of inviting others into my home. I would worry for days that no one would show up. I would fret over cleaning the house. I would fret over the menu. I would be a walking, talking bundle of nerves.

It's Not About the Size

One reason why I was intimidated was because I compared my home to those of my friends. My previous home was comfortable, but not big. It was the farthest away. Because I had young children, my furniture was what we will call well-used. I loved my home, but it wasn't the fanciest by any stretch of the imagination.

The same is true of my rental. While in a more centralized location and closer to my friends, the house is in need of updates. Built in the 1950s, the kitchen and bathroom are original. Picture olive green kitchen cabinets and a bathroom colored more like a nursery with baby pink tiles separating from the walls by age paired with a baby blue commode and matching bathtub. How could this older, smaller, dated home compare to the homes of my friends?

Mary and TC have a beautiful, renovated home on a riverfront in a suburb of Chicago. Linda and Steve gutted their "starter home" in which they have lived for 30+ years, redoing every room, some from the studs out. Charlene lives in a five-bedroom home that is designed so well we all want to live there. Ann and Jack remodeled the farm house in which their children are the sixth generation to live, creating an oasis with a beautiful kitchen and a tv large enough to hang from the roof of a sports arena. My newest friend, Diane, lives in a modern home with a breathtaking view of a wooded park. And don't even get me started on Dar and Jim's house. If I were younger, I'd ask them to adopt me just so I could hang out at their pool.

The good news for me is that building community is not about comparing myself to someone else, or rather comparing what I own to what others own. Building community is about shared memories and hospitality, plain and simple. It's about how people feel in my home, and I always strive to make them feel welcomed.

A Warm Plan B

The last spring I spent in my former home I hosted a Girls' Night Out gathering for my girlfriends. My ABSOLUTE FAVORITE event is a good GNO. The invitation described the theme as "'A Celebration of Mothers' ... the mothers we are, the mothers we have, the mothers who are with us in spirit." I invited everyone to contribute to the theme by bringing two things: a picture of their mother which I hung like a banner using twine and wooden clothes pins, and an item related to the theme for a little show-n-tell activity. I had planned for this to be a patio event, but Mother Nature had other ideas. We gathered inside as the heavens poured rain, eating wonderful foods each person brought. After dining, the nine of us assembled in the den. Seating consisted of plastic chairs brought in when the rain began, an ottoman, kitchen chairs, a love seat and couch.

I began the show-n-tell with a picture and short story of Frances. Everyone in the room had a different relationship with their mothers. Some of my friends are incredibly close to their mothers, while others are not. I wanted to represent the women who, while not our birth mothers, had inspired us. I then held up four small ceramic figurines. One larger frog and a bunny are designed to hold mini tealight candles. Two smaller frogs are sunbathing. All four will fit into one of my hands and can be found as decorations in my bathroom. I then told the following story.

When my son KJ was younger he was diagnosed as asthmatic. His respiratory problems were seasonal and often triggered by the turning of dirt in the seasons of planting or harvesting in our rural area. Usually his biggest attacks came in the fall, but when he was in 5th grade he had an attack which left him hospitalized over Mother's Day weekend. He was discharged that Sunday and we stopped at a local Walgreen's to fill his prescriptions. I was physically and emotionally exhausted having stayed with my son in the hospital. KJ and Gracie were distraught, to the point of tears, that it was Mother's Day and they didn't have any gifts for me. I gave them $10 to spend (the only cash I had) and went to stand by the front door while they shopped. The four figurines I shared at the GNO were bought by my children at that Walgreen's as part of my Mother's Day present. They have always symbolized for me not only the sacrifices we make for our children but the love my son and daughter had in making sure I was gifted. As silly as it sounds, if my house ever catches fire and I need to make a hasty exit, I will grab my purse, car keys, laptop, a few meaningful pictures and these four figurines from the bathroom.

When her turn came, Sharon stood and after showing us a picture of her mother she held up a wireless phone, the kind you set on a landline cradle. She told how she and her mother speak every night on that phone. "What my mother doesn't know is that I don't hang up right away," Sharon said. "I hear the sweetest things when she doesn't know I am listening. Some nights she will say, 'I just love that girl' and it touches my heart."

Dar brought a custom-made ankle brace that was fitted for her mother when she was having trouble walking. Ginny was as stubborn, spirited and independent as they come and even though the brace was not inexpensive she refused to wear it, preferring instead to wear two different sizes of shoes because the larger one made her foot feel better.

One story prompted another which prompted another. Cheryl told of a painting at home which her son Matt made for her. Linda told of the silent chorus signed at her deaf mother's funeral. As the rain poured outside, the warmth between a community of friends gathered in my small den was comforting.

The Gathering Place

Just after Christmas, 2017, my son called me with a request. Several of his former high school buddies were in town and wanted to have a Guys' Night Out. These boys had all been to our house frequently as they were growing up. Dexter is practically my second son. Brody and KJ vied for the starting catcher's position on the JV and Varsity baseball teams, especially in the later years when KJ slimmed down making him more mobile. I sat with Chuckie's mom on the sideline all through pee wee football. Brandon and Tyler had slept on my couch many, many times, as had Zach and Justin. At the time of this request, three of these boys were in the military, one in college, one a firefighter, one attending the police academy and two were working hard to build their careers. I will admit that I always had a sense of accomplishment as a parent knowing that they all felt welcomed in my home. Well, except that one night just before graduation when they were rowdy and loud, causing Gracie and me delayed sleep. My throwing Guitar Hero paraphernalia out the front door at 1:00 a.m. wasn't perhaps my finest moment.

Gracie was home from college the week KJ approached me, asking if I would consider vacating my rental house while he and his buddies had an all-nighter of gaming. "I'll pay for a hotel room for the two of you," he offered. Most parents may think I was crazy to even consider the request, but I knew the boys were mostly harmless; so, I agreed. Besides, it would be nice to have a mini getaway with Gracie. "Thanks," KJ responded. "Just let me know how much the hotel room is and I'll pay for at least half." We were talking on the phone, but I am pretty sure the word "Sucker" appeared on my forehead.

Let me say upfront that I was never a big fan of video games. I know a young man whose parents struggled with what the mom honestly believed was a serious problem with gaming. The more he gamed, the more distant he became. His social circle became smaller and his interest in extra-curricular activities all but disappeared. His grades tanked and his physical health suffered. My own perception with gaming in my home was that it generally was a waste of time and took away from other, more productive activities.

But as KJ and his friends have gotten older, I have gained a new respect for online gaming. Just as with social media, gaming can be positive or negative. These friends who would gather in my home once again were scattered across multiple towns, states and even countries. They stay connected through online gaming. Before KJ moved out, he would often be in the basement gaming and talking to

Dexter in Texas, Chuckie in South Carolina, and Justin in their hometown. It was over this medium that one friend would announce his engagement, another would announce he was getting married and would be a dad, another would reminisce about some event long past. This community of friends, bonded through high school and sports but still connected through online gaming, continues to gather whether virtually or in person. Just as with social media, gaming serves as a mechanism to maintain their friendships. And my house continues to serve as a gathering place when they all make it back home.

It Feels Like Home

For a while, my rental home felt very odd. I was uncomfortable and even at times a bit scared. I had moved from a smaller town to what I like to call "civilization." When people came to visit for the first time, I would take them on a tour of the house, pointing out the things I would fix if I were to buy the place. I could knock out the half wall between the dining area and kitchen to open it up more. I would certainly remodel the nursery/bathroom. I would bring the laundry machines up from the basement. And don't even get me started on the third level which is unfinished and unusable. For several weeks it felt as if I was living in someone else's home, even after I decorated and hung my own pictures.

The tide of discomfort changed when I hosted a Christmas brunch at my home for a group of friends prior to our attending a local holiday home tour. The laughter, chatter and friendship brought a longed-for familiarity and helped to christen what I had come to refer to as my cozy cottage. And I was reminded of one very important thing. A house is not a home because it stores our personal possessions. A house becomes a home when it is filled with love, friendship and memories. Community happens when love and friendship are extended to others. My friends, and KJ's friends, like to come to our home because they know they are always welcomed.

It would be very easy for me to refrain from hosting based on the comparisons I made earlier. My house is older and in need of updates. My house is smaller, etc. Those things don't matter to my friends. We could gather in the bathroom at a nearby pizza joint and have a grand time doing so. Comparisons only hinder opportunities to build community with others.

A lady named Wendy used to tell me, "If you want to see me, drop by any time. If you want to see my house, make an appointment." I cannot count how many times I have quoted that line. But it is so true.

Even after years of hosting parties, I still get caught up in the details of planning. I still fret. I still get anxious. But I have come to cherish the memories made and the expanding community of friends I have gathered along the way. Whether it's a Girls' Night Out, a sports party, cards, or just a quiet dinner with one or two friends, I ABSOLUTELY LOVE building community by inviting others to share time with me in my home.

Chapter 2 Reflection

"No one has seen God at any time. If we love one another, God abides in us, and His love has been perfected in us."
1 John 4:12

Q1: How can comparing what we own to what others own hinder the building of community?

Q2: Hospitality may not be your strong suit. What gifts do you have that allow you to build community with others?

Q3: We all have heard catchy phrases such as "If you want to see me, stop by any time. If you want to see my house, make an appointment." What is a phrase that you have heard that helps keep you grounded in what is important in life? Remember to give credit where credit is due as a way of recognizing someone in your community.

Q4: How would you define hospitality? What synonyms (similar words) can you think of that would also relate to the building of community?

Q5: When was the last time someone extended hospitality to you? How did that make you feel?

Space intentionally left blank for your own thoughts.

Space intentionally left blank for your own thoughts.

~ ~ ~

Focus of Chapter 3:

When we risk being vulnerable or transparent with others, the result can be humbling. I experienced this personally after I began telling a story I hadn't told in over 30 years. As you read of my experience, consider times you have connected with someone else when the fear of being vulnerable was overcome.

~ ~ ~

Chapter 3: Have I Got a Story for You!

Transparent

As I mentioned earlier, I have recently become involved in MOTH storytelling. Below you will find two of my scripts for those stories, to give you an idea of what I have shared. These are what I consider to be two of my better attempts.

Topic: Love Hurts, February 2017

Tonight, I want to introduce you to a member of my family named Roscoe. He is a mixture between a Shih Tzu and a poodle and basically, he's the perfect sized lap dog.

Roscoe is a great co-pilot. He LOVES riding in the car, especially when taking the kids to school.

He is an awesome nursemaid. I don't care if you are sick for 24 hours or 6 weeks after surgery, Roscoe is right there by your side.

Roscoe is a fearless protector of the home. If he hears another dog outside, he will immediately run out and begin barking at the offending canine. After he barks awhile he will turn, lift his leg, pee on the other dog and come back inside. Now, I would think this would offend the other dog, but apparently it doesn't because this same ritual repeats itself time and time again.

Roscoe is VERY schedule oriented. At precisely 8:40 PM he will hunt you down to tell you it's time for his nightly dingo (rawhide bone). *When you give it to him he takes the dingo, throws it in the air, and watches it fall. He'll slam it against the wall, and watch it fall. He runs around the bone barking, letting the inanimate object know that not only is he king of the backyard he is also king of the living room. Then he will roll around on top of the bone, making it smell like himself. Then, and only then will he proceed to eat the bone which, if you think about it, is slightly cannibalistic.*

Now, I chose to tell the first part of this story in present tense, even though Roscoe no longer lives with me. In May 2016, I was going through some life transitions and I simply couldn't take care of Roscoe anymore. The thought broke my heart. But through what I believe to be Divine intervention I met an older, retired woman named Ann who was looking for a new pet. (For reader clarification, this is not the same Ann referenced elsewhere in this book. The names are coincidental.)

When Ann and I met for the pre-adoption home study, she asked me several questions about grooming and his shot history. She then asked me "Does Roscoe like ice cream?" In that moment, even as my heart was breaking, I knew that my dog was going to love living with Ann.

When I took Roscoe back to drop him off, I walked in and couldn't say a word. Roscoe was on his leash, so Ann took him to the backyard so he could find new dogs to pee on. I left an industrial-sized bag of dingos on the table, along with a piece of my heart, and walked away.

I told you that Roscoe is a member of my family; he still is. We may have parents who get older and move to a retirement community, or children who grow up and go to college. That doesn't make them any less a part of our family. For me, it's easier to think Roscoe has moved to his retirement home, as opposed to his being gone forever.

Topic: Gifts Given, December 2017

I believe that one of the greatest gifts that we can give to each other is the sharing of our stories. I was reminded of this on November 5 as I was sitting in church.

Many of you know that November is national adoption awareness month. In the church that I attend we have 4 families who have adopted children. Three of them were first foster families who adopted children born to mothers with drug addictions. One of them adopted a child from a birth mother who was 15 years old. So, I sat there, listening to these stories and just sensed that something was missing. Adopted families were represented. One young lady who was adopted spoke. But, something was missing.

Now, what happened next is hard for me to explain because unless you were sitting in my chair I don't think you will understand the gravity of what I did next. You know how you get in your car and drive someplace familiar, like work or the grocery store, and you remember getting in the car, and you know you arrived at your destination, but you don't remember anything in between? That's what happened to me that morning. One minute I am in my seat at church, and the next minute I am up on stage whispering to the pastor ... right in the middle of the service! I looked him in the eye and said, "The one voice that you do not have represented this morning is the voice of someone who gave a child up for adoption." He nodded somewhat affirmatively, and I went on to say, "I am that voice." And then I found myself with a microphone in my hand, telling a story that I do not tell often ... not because I am ashamed or hiding something ... it just isn't a story that

I share often and have NEVER shared publicly like I did that morning. I can honestly tell you that in the 31 years since I made that decision I have never once had a moment of regret and that's because adoption was absolutely the right choice for me. I was simply a good kid in college who hooked up with a good kid in college and got pregnant. I wasn't ready to be a parent and I wasn't ready to be married. So, I chose adoption.

After I told my story I went back to my seat and a few people around me patted my back and briefly hugged me. Later, I was walking out amid the crowd and a woman that I do not know, who does not sit near me usually, grabbed my arm, looked intently into my eyes and simply said two words ... "Thank you." And as she did this, our eyes held, and it was one of those moments where you can see the other person's heart reflected in their eyes. And I knew, at that moment, that this woman had her own story to tell. But she didn't have to, because in some way I had given her experience a voice.

You could say that 31 years ago I gave two people an incredible gift by entrusting them with the care of the child to whom I had given birth. And I agree with that. It took a lot of courage on my part to do that. And in a totally different way, it took a lot of courage for me that November morning to get up and share what I did in church. I came off that platform physically shaking – but within just a few minutes I knew that I had given that woman who grabbed my arm a rare gift ... I had shared my story and in doing so gave HER story recognition.

A Bar, Two Prayers, and A Hug

Telling that second story has done more to help me create community than maybe anything else I have done. In doing so, I have had to open a few closed doors from my past and in my heart. As I have discussed what happened that Sunday morning with my close friends, several of them have pondered whether I am being prepared for something, perhaps a young man seeking me out after 31 years. I have responded each time that, at the moment, it doesn't feel that way. It feels more like I was meant to be open to saying what I said that Sunday morning, and then later as part of the open mic storytelling. It feels like the story is the tool being used.

In early February, Bryan, the host from the local storytelling group, and I drove to Detroit, Michigan to attend and hopefully compete in a MOTH event. We had missed the online ticket sales, so we had to stand outside for 40 minutes in the cash line – not knowing if we could even get into the building. It was below zero with gusting winds and light snow flurries. It was just plain frigid. Not everyone in the cash line got in that night, but at the last minute Bryan and I did. Parts of my body were numb as we paid the cover charge and literally ran to the front of the venue to get our names in the drawing for storytellers before the show began. I am not one to fly by the seat of my pants too often, but this night was exhilarating.

The venue, called the Marble Bar, was packed bumper to bumper with people. The rows of chairs were tight and people were standing all around the room. Bryan and I moved stage left and stood at the end of the bar where there was at least some breathing room. I didn't mind standing given the seven hours of driving we would be doing that night. And standing allowed my frozen blood to thaw and flow again.

Fourteen storytellers had put their names in the drawing that night and only 10 would be chosen. Our odds were good, but not assured. The lineup would be five storytellers, intermission, and then another five stories. After the fourth storyteller was announced, I simply looked up at the ceiling and sent a quick message to God. "If you want my story to be told tonight, I'm ready. If not, that's ok, too." My name was drawn fifth.

I stepped on stage and greeted the crowd, confessing I had never been to Detroit before. I then told my story, the same adoption story I shared earlier. This night the topic was again "Love Hurts." In Dayton I had used my Roscoe story for this topic, but on this night I went with what was quickly becoming my most powerful story. The ending changed to match the topic and went like this:

Since that Sunday morning in November, I have had to sort through a lot of emotions. I was so overwhelmed by the intense feeling I had that I needed to speak up that morning. I have been humbled by the thought that my stories can have an impact on someone, just like the lady who thanked me. And, to be honest, I have had to revisit some of the emotions I felt in college when I made the choice to put a child up for adoption. Loving a child enough to make that decision does not come without pain, certainly at the time that it happens, and sometimes ... 31 years later.

As I exited the stage, the applause was genuine. I was on a high and ready to go back to my little corner to catch my breath. After my scores were announced, I was leading going into intermission. Always after I tell a good story people will come up to me and congratulate me and express their appreciation. Not going to lie, that is pretty cool. But here is where the story gets EVEN COOLER.

Sitting in the second row, stage left was a lady who I will call Woman #1. We exchanged names, but I will not give hers in case what she told me is confidential. As I left the stage, people were standing for the break and milling around. Woman #1 grabbed my hand as if to shake it and wouldn't let go. I was caught up in the moment of being on stage and leading and wanted to move to the side to do an internal "boo-yah!" I didn't want to hold this stranger's hand. I didn't want to be stopped. I glanced at her face and she was smiling slightly and nodding affirmatively. I thought she was simply touched by my story. As I pulled away I looked at her again and there it was – that look – the same one I had gotten in early November when I was thanked at church by another nameless woman. Before I could react, I got caught up in the crowd and our hands separated. I moved to the side and my "boo-yah" moment had passed. I had something I needed to do.

I went to an opening at the bar, thanking several people in route who told me they liked my story. I ordered a beer, took a deep breath, and headed back toward the hand-holding lady. I acted as if I was surveying the crowd looking for someone, intentionally moving closer to her right side. I started the conversation simply.

"Is this place always this packed?" I asked. "Every time," she responded. I then took a sip of my drink and simply looked back into her face, not in a hurry this time. Her eyes began to tear.

"I was really moved by your story."

"Thank you. I appreciate that," I replied.

"I know you get told that a lot," she said. "You're a good storyteller."

"Thank you. I appreciate that."

She moved in closer. "My mom put a child up for adoption before she had me," Woman #1 said. Boo-yah moment had come back, but not the same as before. Better this time, much better.

"I thought you had a story," I said. She didn't offer any more details. She didn't have to. Our connection was grounded. "I'm Sandra," I said as I extended my hand. She gave me her name in return.

This time the handshake was more familiar, not so hurried. We chatted about storytelling in general and a little about Detroit. At least I think we did. I honestly don't remember much about the small talk. All I knew was that I was humbled yet again. BUT WAIT, the story gets EVEN BETTER.

I spoke with another storyteller before going back to my corner at the bar, getting patted on the back and thanked as I navigated the crowd. Once I was back in my spot where I would stand for the last five storytellers, another lady sought me out. I will call her Woman #2.

"I was very touched by your story," she said. I made eye contact, this time a pro at knowing "the look."

"Thank you, I appreciate that," I responded.

"My mother was adopted," my new community member said. "She died four months ago. I have been thinking about her a lot and just moved for months by gratitude for the woman who gave life to my mother. If she had made a different choice, my family wouldn't be here." I nodded, not wanting to interrupt.

She went on. "My mother never wanted to find her birth mother. But I just feel like I would like to give her a hug and say 'Thanks.'"

"Well, if it's alright with you," I said, stifling my own emotions, "I'll take that hug on her behalf."

The woman's eyes sparkled, partly from moisture and mostly from gratitude. We embraced, and I silently looked back up at the ceiling with another silent prayer, this one even shorter. "Thank you."

Recognition and Willingness

The reactions I am getting from strangers when I tell this story are so amazing and humbling for me. I have also been humbled by the reaction of my friends when I tell them the whole story of what happened in college. As I said, I have rarely told my story. Many who are closest to me had never heard it before. What is cool is the fact that I am connecting with friends on a level we never experienced before because they, too, have their own stories to tell.

One friend had a false alarm when she thought she was pregnant in high school and she remembers thinking that she would have terminated the pregnancy because her parents would have thrown her out of the house. Another friend shared that a friend in high school was indeed forced out by her parents when she got pregnant, so she chose adoption as well. Others shared of their own choices made. Not all my friends could relate to my story of adoption. But every time I shared it, always one-on-one, I walked away knowing that I was that much closer to the person with whom I had shared. There is a certain connection that is made when we are transparent and open ourselves to being vulnerable to one another.

If you think my stories are moving, you should hear some of the other tellers who present. I am in awe of several of the regular storytellers who do open mic each month. For Nathan's "Love Hurts" story, he told of shunning a girl in high school in favor of pursuing other interests, only to find out that the girl was his dream come true several years later. His wife Tracy sat in the audience in support of her husband and we all were moved along with her. Kayla began one story by describing the birth of her son who had to be brought back to life with an ice bath when his heart stopped. Bridget has a Me Too story that will bring you to tears and takes courage to tell. Each time those stories are told, community happens.

Stories lead to recognition of shared experiences and a willingness to trust the listener, and those two things are what build communities. The stories are simply a conduit for the connection to happen.

Open to Opportunities

When I went through my first divorce, I was attending a large United Methodist Church. The church had what was called a HUGS network. I remember the acronym, but not what it stood for. The idea was to encourage connection between people who had similar experiences. When I became divorced, Wendy, the woman who may or may not clean her house if you are coming over, reached out and asked if I wanted to go to dinner. Having two very young children, I had some logistics to work out to have a free night, but we eventually connected. I was a little leery to be honest, until Wendy suggested that we meet at The Thirsty Dog for a relaxing and casual meal. That short venture into the world of adults with a woman who herself had been divorced and left to raise her son was like being thrown a life preserver. We lingered to the extent I was able, sharing stories and connecting over shared experiences. I haven't seen Wendy in years, but the memory of that experience is still worthy of note.

Each of us has come to this day in our lives carrying stories that make us who we are. I have found that sharing those stories with others is a powerful way to build community. For me, the important thing has been to be open to opportunities to engage others in conversation and share common experiences. Being transparent and vulnerable is scary and hard. Just like many other things, each time we open up to others it gets a little easier. It doesn't matter if you are on stage, interrupting a church service, or hanging out in a restaurant – if you take the opportunity to share your story with others, I guarantee you will be amazed at the connections which occur.

Chapter 3 Reflection

"You are the light of the world. A city built on a hill cannot be hid. No one after lighting a lamp puts it under the bushel basket, but on the lampstand, and it gives light to all in the house. In the same way, let your light shine before others, so that they may see your good works and give glory to your Father in heaven." Matthew 5:14-16

Q1: If it were allowable to do so, I would take the scripture reference above and change the ending to read "... let your light shine before others, so that they may add their own light to yours and flood the entire city and give glory to your Father in heaven." Describe the feelings you have when you discover an unknown connection with someone.

Q2: When have you been afraid to share something personal at the risk of being vulnerable? How did you overcome your fear? What happened?

Q3: Not everyone is accepting of our vulnerabilities. What barriers have you experienced to people being transparent with one another?

Q4: For those of you adding scripture to your study, what other passages come to mind that empower you to take a leap of faith and share your own stories with others?

Space intentionally left blank for your own thoughts.

~ ~ ~

Focus of Chapter 4:

The word "community" has many different connotations. My main focus is on the sense of community that we feel when we connect with others. In this chapter, I share short stories about the people who live in my physical community. I do this to continue conversation on ways we can support one another, regardless of our zip code.

~ ~ ~

Chapter 4: Won't You Be My Neighbor?

Supportive

Having lived in my previous home for 16 years, I knew everyone who lived on my street. Shoot, the town was so small I knew just about everyone who drove down my street. If you turned right two houses west of me, you would be headed toward the school system, the local park and the football/soccer stadium. My street was well traveled.

A Helping Hand

At the far end of the street lived Bruce and Edith. Bruce was retired from GM and my family always called him the Lawnmower Man. In his retirement he would buy or swap old lawnmowers, refurbish them, and then sell them for a small profit. He would also fix lawnmowers, giving them a seasonal tune-up each spring. Edith always had such lovely flowers in her beds and you would often see the two sitting on their front porch, ready to engage in conversation. Bruce died very unexpectedly one day after falling off a ladder. When he died, it seemed as if Edith moved inside permanently. Flowers wilted and the beds became overgrown. Neighbors stepped in and began to mow her grass without being asked. Grief can be isolating. People in community understand this. They don't wait to be asked to help. They see a need and respond accordingly.

Mrs. Claus

Bev and Robert were original residents of the road when

the development was first being built. Bev spends more time in her yard than anyone on the street. She cuts her grass every 2.5 days it seems. She grows flowers and vegetables and other plants that I can't even categorize. She often sits on a bench swing in her backyard, enjoying the beauty she has created. This obviously brings her joy.

For several years, Bev brought joy to my family. When my children were young and I was a single parent, we had a tradition of going to Christmas Eve service at 6:00 and then coming home to find that Santa had delivered our presents. I took advantage of the notion that "Santa has to start somewhere" on his worldwide trip. Many times, Bev played the role of Mrs. Claus, delivering presents while we were at church. This tactic by the way also allowed my children to believe in Santa a few years longer than they might have otherwise. How could I possibly be Santa if I was at church with them when the presents were delivered? Clever Mama.

One year it snowed 20 inches and service was cancelled. What to do now? I fretted and pouted, afraid this tradition would be spoiled. In the end, the kids and I made a quick trip to McDonald's, literally the only business open in our small town. As we ate, I was near tears. I was trying so hard to make special memories for my children and now one of the most important was jeopardized. I had plans for a pot of homemade soup and fresh bread for dinner; instead we were eating chicken nuggets and fries. We must have seemed pitiful to the restaurant staff, a lone mother and her children eating in a fast food restaurant on Christmas Eve. When we returned home, Bev had made her way through the snow and delivered the presents. Somehow, she had even managed to cover her footprints so it wasn't obvious a neighbor two doors down had come into the house. KJ and Gracie's excitement and joy were equal to years past, perhaps even a bit greater. Not only did Santa know we normally went to church, he even knew when we came home earlier than expected!

As simple as it sounds, Bev played a very important role for me. Knowing that the kids would leave on Christmas mornings to visit the paternal side of their family, I cherished the opportunity to celebrate the night before. If I had waited and done the more traditional present exchange on Christmas mornings as the children awoke, we would have had only a short time to appreciate our gifts. I never could have pulled this off for my children with the same level of amazement and wonder without Bev's assistance.

Years later, as a surprise to us, Bev left in our mailbox every letter to Santa that the kids had left on the table over the years. It brought tears to my eyes that she had kept them all. Neighbors in community recognize that families come in all shapes and sizes and need help pulling off surprises. They even sometimes trek through 20 inches of snow to deliver a Dora the Explorer doll that allows a young girl to proclaim with excitement, "Santa knew exactly what I wanted!"

Timing Is Everything

The first neighbors I met when I moved to the block were Carol and Slick. The husband's name was Elvira, but the nickname fit him to a tee. Slick came over to the moving truck before I had even climbed out of the cab to welcome me to the neighborhood. Carol and Slick lived in a tri-level with a gorgeous inground pool. As I prepared to marry a second time, a union which involved six children between us – five of whom would live with us initially – I looked with Dave, my fiancé, at the tri-level as Carol and Slick were ready to downsize. This was in 2008 when the housing market tanked. We had hoped to sell two houses and buy the larger one, which in the end never happened. Carol and Slick waited for 10 months and might have waited longer I suppose if Slick hadn't had a fatal aneurism in the lower level of the home. Carol sold the house and moved closer to her daughter. In the end, Dave lost his job six months after we wed and took the opportunity to go back to school for two years to complete his degree. If we had bought the larger house with the larger mortgage we would have been sunk financially. Neighbors in community are willing to wait and do something nice for one another, until fate determines otherwise.

It's a Dog's World

For a long time, I lived next to a family that I will simply say was very not nice. Rarely are communities perfect. Luckily, when they departed the sweetest young couple moved in, Steffi and Gavin (pronounced Gay-vin) and their dog Roo. Soon Cade would join the family as we all celebrated a new baby on the street. After Dave and I divorced, Steffi would go into the house during the mornings to take my Roscoe out. This was a tremendous help. Roo and Roscoe loved each other. The two canines would meet up at one end of our shared fence, stare at each other, and then as if a silent whistle had blown, simultaneously run the length of the fence racing one another. Since Roo is a Siberian Husky and Roscoe a breed with shorter legs, she had an advantage. But what Roscoe lost in stride he made up for with a boundless energy to repeat that same drill over and over and over again. I think Roo mourned as much as I did when Roscoe moved. That's what communities do, they celebrate changes and miss one another when apart.

What's Your Name Again?

When I moved, I lost the sense of community that occurs when you live next to people for such a long period of time. Because my previous home was on a busy thoroughfare, there was constant activity. Even so, given the more populated area to which I had moved, I was expecting my new street to be noisier and busier. It wasn't. I moved in early October, just as the seasons were changing and the days were getting shorter. People were starting to hibernate, which did not provide many opportunities for interaction. I kept telling myself I needed to reserve judgment on how much community there was among my neighbors. I was a newcomer and I needed to be patient.

Before I moved in, a friend came to help me do a few chores. As we walked into the backyard, discovering how quiet and peaceful it was, my southern neighbor-to-be was in her front yard. I broached conversation by commenting on the weather. Patty came over, introduced herself and we chatted for a few moments. She was relatively new to the area as well. After sharing initial information, we went our separate ways. Over the next two months I only saw Patty a couple of times in passing, once inside a nearby strip mall. I was walking past a storefront as Patty was exiting. I backpedaled and said "Neighbor?" She laughed and admitted she had forgotten my name. We re-introduced ourselves and chatted for a moment.

Thanksgiving came and went, as did Christmas. Two days after Christmas there was a card in my mail slot addressed simply "Neighbors." It was from Patty. She wished me and my son a happy new year and admitted that she had again forgotten my name. When I next saw her outside I thanked her for the card and reintroduced myself for a third time, making us both chuckle. I told Patty that KJ was moving, making me an official Empty Nester. She suggested coffee sometime since we both live alone.

As spring began to take hold and lawns started growing, I began to see Patty more often. One night she was afraid to go inside her house after leaving the garage door open. She came and knocked on my door and I accompanied her on a quick investigation to make sure all was safe. When her lawnmower died, I offered mine as a temporary tool until hers could be fixed. One afternoon I locked myself out of the house. Patty drove me to my son so I could get his set of keys. Little by little we are becoming more acquainted. And little by little I am meeting others on my street.

An Unexpected Encounter

I met another neighbor somewhat by chance. An hour after I finished writing the first draft of this chapter, I left my house to go to a University of Dayton Women's Basketball game. I will admit that in the 21 years that I have lived in or near Dayton I had never been to a UD Women's basketball game. I was joining a MeetUp group that I had never met. I needed the break from writing to recharge my battery.

As I got in my car, I noticed a neighbor across the street getting into his truck. He had on a distinctive sweatshirt and a red, white and blue toboggan hat. UD's colors are red, white and blue. I thought to myself: wouldn't it be a nice postscript to this chapter I have just written if I (a) met one of my neighbors by chance at (b) an activity that I have never been to before which (c) I was attending with a group that I have never joined before?

Well, that afternoon I intentionally looked during the game for the man I had seen and took the opportunity to introduce myself as a means of building community. We chatted for a few moments between quarters. The fact that the guy knew enough about our neighbors to fill me in on a few served as a good sign that I may not have such a hard time meeting people around me after all. Time will tell.

A Means of Support

Neighbors are supportive of one another, whether that be through mowing someone's grass, tending to a pet, or answering the call when someone says, "I hate to bother you, but would you mind ..." Building community takes time and patience. It also takes being supportive of others through all of life's challenges.

Chapter 4 Reflection

"The first of all the commandments is: 'You shall love the Lord your God with all your heart, and with all your soul, with all your mind, and with all your strength.' And the second is this: 'You shall love your neighbor as yourself.' There is no other commandment greater than these."
Mark 12:29-31

Q1: What friend or family member have you lost to death? Who stepped in to fill the void, much as neighbors did when Edith needed someone to mow her yard? Perhaps you know someone who has suffered a loss. How can you help?

Q2: Think of the physical communities around you: where you live, where you work, where you attend church or participate in a favorite pastime. Describe why you feel a sense of community in those places.

Q3: The emphasis word chosen for this chapter is "Supportive." Name three verbs that you consider to be synonymous with support. How do those actions come into play when we consider building community with one another?

Space intentionally left blank for your own thoughts.

~ ~ ~

Focus of Chapter 5:

In this chapter, I suggest, "Perhaps the greatest gift we can give to others in our attempt to build community is that of hope in the form of compassion." We experience hope and compassion in different ways, such as when we share each other's grief. As you read, consider how simple words or acts of compassion can impact others or have impacted you.

~ ~ ~

Chapter 5: There for Ya'

Compassionate

It has been very interesting how several of the chapters in this book came to be. I struggled with this one, rewriting it several times. I went to bed one night thinking I had a final version. That night I slept for maybe two hours before waking up restless. I streamed a movie, went back to bed, and had a moment of sudden clarity. I then got up and typed for two hours as I completely rewrote the greater part of this chapter.

That same flash of inspiration has occurred often as I share my writing talent with others. Over the years I have presented my friends with gifts of words. I call these "creations" for lack of a better term. They are prose but have a certain rhythm to them. They don't always rhyme, but most have a certain style that I have incorporated. These are only meaningful because I know the recipient personally. I couldn't mass market my creations because each one is unique.

I am going to share with you two of the creations I have gifted because they represent grief, love and compassion, all universal emotions. There are underlying meanings to the words, which only the recipient will understand. But, you will get a flavor of what I have created.

I wrote *Tap, Tap, Tap* and presented it to Scott after his mother, Mary Lee, passed away. Scott is an accomplished actor, singer and tap dancer.

Tap .. Tap .. Tap ..
The beat of a newborn son's heart,
Precious … Loved … Held

> *Tap .. Tap .. Tap ..*
> The beat of a new mother's heart,
> Anxious … Joy-filled … Learning

Tap .. Tap .. Tap ..
The beat of a youthful man's heart,
Energetic … Head-strong … Willful

> *Tap .. Tap .. Tap ..*
> The beat of a strong mother's heart,
> Teaching … Guiding … Praying

Tap .. Tap .. Tap ..
The beat of a man's heart,
Talented … Wiser … Grateful

> *Tap .. Tap ..*
> The beat of an ill mother's heart,
> Proud … Weak … Silent

Tap ..
The beat of a grieving son's heart,
Precious … Loved … Held

Tap .. Tap ..
The beat of a determined man's heart,
Teaching … Dancing … Remembering.

A Mother's Love

It is so hard to watch a friend grieve the loss of a family member. Your heart aches for them and you don't know how to help. My friend Ann's mother and father lived together in a retirement community. Her father had more profound signs of aging: chronic pain, loss of mobility, loss of hearing, some cognitive impairment. I think the family thought he would die first. What they didn't understand was how much Ann's mother was doing for her husband. The toll of being a caregiver is hard. Marilyn died one week after Mother's Day in 2017.

When Marilyn died, Ann and her siblings had to jump in and care for dad. This involved a move, coordinating doctor's appointments and in-home care. When someone dies, there is a lot of business that must be handled. Add to that caring for the second parent, and you quickly realize that grief must be put on hold. For several months I witnessed the toll this took on Ann. Seven or eight months after Marilyn passed away, Ann attended a grief care class where she learned that grief is hard because it is not a moment in time event. Every day brings a trigger reminding you of your loss, like holidays when someone is missing at the table. There are moments when you think, "I'm making mom's recipe. What was that special ingredient she used? I'll call and ask her. ... Oh, wait, I can't."

Ann and her mom shared a love of gardening and music. At the funeral visitation, several friends presented Ann with two peonies to plant in her garden. Marilyn played piano and organ at church for decades and had a library of sheet music. Upon her death, Ann kept a few special pieces, but donated the rest to an organist at a local church. The first Mother's Day that Ann spent without her mom, she decided she would go to church where that organist was playing. He played two of Marilyn's pieces. As Ann told me the story later, she said, "I sat there listening. I looked up at the stained-glass windows and there was such a lovely light coming through. I knew mom was smiling down."

Shared Grief

Just before Christmas in 2017, another friend lost her mother. Charlene's mom was 96 years old and had lived independently until moving to assisted living at the age of 94. Charlene and her mom wrote letters to each other and talked weekly. Charlene spoke of this when she shared her story at my Mother's Day GNO earlier in 2017. In addition to her grief, Charlene had to deal with some anger at the loss of her mother because there were extenuating circumstances involved.

One night, Dar, Charlene and I went together to a play based on the life of Erma Bombeck. Afterwards, we came back to my home and ate a second round of dessert as we sat in the living room and chatted. The topic of losing one's mother came up and Charlene shared with Dar some of her story. Dar lost her mom in 2013, and as they talked you could tell her grief had not dissipated much. I sat back and listened, as two ladies who are part of my community but only know each other through me shared their grief and compassion for one another.

Universal Emotions

Grief is not limited to the loss of a mother or loved one. People grieve the loss of a job, a pet, a marriage. I found this out the hard way.

As I mentioned earlier, there is a lot of business that occurs after the death of a family member. The same is true after a divorce. When I first divorced, my children were very young. That year I also moved and had a job change, so my life was hectic to say the least. I got busy taking care of my family and daily logistics. I did not have time to deal with nuisances such as emotions and grieving.

Fast forward seven years to 2005. I ventured briefly back into the dating world and after a short, six-week relationship I found myself emotionally distraught. My breakdown spanned several weeks when during the day I would function in such a way that no one would guess I was having any issues. But I would end each evening, after putting my children to bed on my couch, curled up in a fetal position, sobbing and crying for hours. And the worst part was … I had no idea why.

I tried prescribed anti-depressants, but had some pretty crazy side effects with those, so I gave up on meds. I sought counseling and unbeknownst to me the guy I went to was an expert on the subject of grief. As we got into counseling, he shared his opinion that I was grieving the loss of my marriage. What? Not this lady. I thought the counselor was nuts. Seriously, trust me. There was no way in the world I was grieving my divorce from my ex-husband. On the contrary; I was relieved to not be married to him. I almost quit going to this counselor.

But then, as we talked more, I realized he was right. Over the years I have reflected on that time and have come to understand three things about grief and anger. First, these two strong emotions cannot be ignored. If you try, they will come back and bite you in the backside at some point. Secondly, grief and anger can be a catalyst to something good. In 2015, as my second marriage was coming to an end, I walked and/or ran over 1000 miles that calendar year. Over the miles, I reflected, cried and even screamed at times. This helped me avoid the past mistake of ignoring my emotions.

Third and maybe the most important thing I learned, and am reminded of with the stories of Ann, Dar and Charlene, is that grief and anger are universal emotions. We all have experienced grief. We all have been angry. And when we compassionately share those experiences with each other our burdens become lighter.

Compassionate Hope

Perhaps the greatest gift we can give to others in our attempt to build community is that of hope in the form of compassion. We may do that with a planted flower that when in bloom reminds the recipient of not only her mother but friends who continue to be "there for ya'." We do that with spoken words, maybe on a couch after a play while sharing gluten-free coconut cookie bars. I attempt to do that with my creations, such as this one that I wrote for Ann which I presented to her at Christmas, having taken a few months to get the words just right. It is titled *You Will Find Her, She Is Near*.

Day after day, year after year,
You will find her; she is near.

She is by you as you sew with needle and thread.
She is with you on your knees in your flowerbed.

She is smiling down as you rock your grandchild.
She is holding your dad's hand as you sit with him awhile.

She is in the lyrics and melody of a memorable song.
She is in the traditions that you and your family carry on.

She is there in the simplest of your daily tasks.
She is there in the answers to the questions you ask.

She is nearby as your grief is powerful and strong.
She is in the midst of your celebrations, laughing along.

She is in you, in your heart and in your mind.
She is the spirit that a mother leaves behind.

Day after day, year after year,
You will find her; she is near.

Chapter 5 Reflection

As God's chosen ones, holy and beloved, clothe yourselves with compassion, kindness, humility, meekness, and patience. Bear with one another and, if anyone has a complaint against another, forgive each other; just as the Lord has forgiven you, so you also must forgive.
Colossians 3:12-13 (NRSV)

Q1: Think back to a time when you were grieving. What emotions do you remember being the strongest at the time?

Q2: A search for synonyms for compassion resulted in sympathy, empathy, concern and kindness. Which of those words strike a chord with you? Why?

Q3: Think back to a time when you and another person engaged in conversation about a shared experience. What was the result of that conversation?

Space intentionally left blank for your own thoughts.

~ ~ ~

Focus of Chapter 6:

We are all busy, focused on our own lives and schedules. We have numerous excuses to not volunteer, to not help someone in need. In reading this, know that I am as guilty as anyone in that regard. At the same time, I have experienced firsthand how humbling it can be when we become aware of someone in need and respond. I will warn you now, you may need a tissue near the end of this longer chapter as you consider ways you can help others simply by becoming aware of their needs.

~ ~ ~

Chapter 6: Spreading Sonshine

Aware

Another place I see people spreading hope is a small town in Southwest Ohio. Germantown is not large, only 5,500 citizens. It is very community-oriented, with Saturday-night-out events in the summer and the annual Pretzel Festival in the fall. The high school football team is perennially in the playoffs and a local community pool sits behind the city government offices, adjacent to a park which has a train caboose at one end. "Shop Local" is a phrase heard often by citizens, who must travel almost 15 miles to find the nearest Wal-Mart or Target.

Feeding the Hungry

I attend church in Germantown. Even after moving I drive back because of the relationships I have there. A few years ago, one member of the congregation, Angi, had it in her heart to begin a program for children in the local schools who were food deficient at home. As a result, every two weeks volunteers pack food into bags which are then distributed to students. In the fall and winter of 2017-2018 we were packing for 180 kids. The program is called "Sonshine in a Bag," hence the name for this chapter. It blows my mind that so many families are food deficient in a town like Germantown, which on the surface appears to be "picture perfect."

Because Angi recognized a need and acted upon it, she is serving the community in which she lives through the church in which she worships utilizing a band of volunteers among which a sense of community is formed. Many lives are touched in the process.

I feel a sense of community when I walk into that hall on Tuesday nights. The volunteers rotate weekly. Two constants are Geri and Bonnie, self-proclaimed "Bag Ladies." The most they can do because of age-related physical limitations is sit and double up the plastic bags we use for bundling food. Well, not exactly "the most" they can do. They quietly inspire others through their unspoken message of "I may not be able to walk far, but my hands work just fine, so I'll offer those." They greet each volunteer and engage them in conversation. Several of the volunteers have physical impairments of their own. Judy has MS. Angi came one week to oversee the operation having just been released from the hospital hours prior due to asthma and severe migraines. There are many weeks when I admittedly go more out of a sense of responsibility than serving. Many excuses are thwarted during the day. But I can honestly say that when I go, I am blessed and inspired not only because I, too, am serving the community but because I need the sense of community I feel in knowing that I am part of something of value. Bonnie, Geri, Angi, and Judy all have far more valid excuses to not be present than I do. But we all need that sense of community.

Fighting Addiction

Another person who has answered the call to serve the Germantown community is Shannon, a vocal part of a coalition to address the ever-growing issue of opioid addiction which is rampant in our part of Ohio. I can't speak much about the coalition or their efforts because I am not directly involved. But I did want to give a shout out to those who are. I wonder what common characteristics are present in people who suffer from harmful addictions. Is it a lack of a sense of community that leaves them feeling isolated? Is it the addiction itself which isolates the individual? I know that opioid addiction is a different matter in that it involves overly prescribed drugs which have a medical side effect. I can only surmise that some of the feelings of isolation are the same as with alcohol or heroin. Shame must play a part for those who are trying to hide the addiction. Shame is a huge obstacle to overcome for those seeking to be part of a community, coupled with fears of not being accepted and of disappointing others. An addiction creeps up on you and you're not even aware there is a problem until the addiction takes hold. At that point, community becomes even more important.

Stepping Up

Another shout out goes to Jack, who with my friend Ann own a local furniture store just outside of Germantown. You know how every local community has a "character" of sorts that everyone knows? That's Jack. As I depart from his presence he will often say, "Sandra, I'm glad you got to see me." If you enter the store to quickly look at a refrigerator or end table you are considering buying, plan on packing a lunch. Jack will talk your ear off. But that's not why he earned a mention in this chapter.

Jack truly cares about people. He does business the old-fashioned way – by listening to what the customer wants and can afford, doing research to find the best value for the money, and even letting some pay off their bill monthly rather than using a credit card, which he doesn't accept anyway. I don't know how many times I have seen him post on the store's Facebook page something like, "I heard there was a fire on the edge of town. Anyone know the family involved? Do they need anything?" Ok, it may be his daughter Jenna or wife who does the actual posting as I am not sure Jack knows how to technically use social media. Whatever method used, Jack is the first one to step up with an offer of assistance.

When I walk into his store I experience a sense of community. His walls are adorned with pictures of local sports teams that he financially supports or students from whom he buys a cow at the county fair. Customers see these as Jack takes the time to sit with them in recliners just shooting the breeze. Any time we are together, I am always glad he got to see me, too.

A Call to Action

Like many other involved citizens and parents, Jack coached his daughters' sports teams over the years. I did the same. My coaching style was more of cheerleader than drill sergeant. I always tried to focus on praising the players and making them better people. I took great pride in small accomplishments. Don't get me wrong – if we could beat Brookville or West Alexandria I was pumped. But what I enjoyed more was the ability to help others that I met through my involvement in sports.

(DISCLAIMER: The story I am going to tell next begins with a few "I" comments. This is not an "I" segment. Please look at this as encouragement for YOU to look around and see how YOU can help others who are in need. In the story "I" quickly turned into "WE" in a matter of minutes and hours. End of disclaimer.)

I first met Steve, Leslie and their daughters Kaitlyn and Brooke as I was coaching basketball through the Upward program at the local Baptist church. Brooke was always one of my favorite athletes, especially in basketball. Neither she nor her sister Katie were the strongest athletically. The story I always tell about Brooke is how her face looked when she rebounded the ball. She would grab the ball, stick her elbows out to ward off the defense, and immediately take on the most intimidating "game face." Seriously, she would look at you like "This is MY ball. You will not take MY ball. I have the ball and it is MY ball." Looking at her in general the word "fierce" would never come to your mind, unless she had HER ball.

Brooke had a similar face when playing defense in soccer. Not the fastest of foot; not the most agile. But if the opposition made eye contact, the intimidation factor alone allowed our team to prevent a score. It was during one soccer season that Steve's health began to decline.

Steve has Cushing's Disease. Never heard of it? Neither had I. Cushing's is hard to diagnose and it took a long time for doctors to put a name on this disease that was slowly sapping Steve's energy. Steve served in the military and was pursuing a promising technology career. Had his story gone any different direction, his family would be financially comfortable. But that hasn't been the case. Steve has a rare form of Cushing's. The associated tumor has grown back multiple times. Cushing's not only saps your energy, but it causes extreme weight gain, lack of mobility and breaks down your bones due to the inability to absorb calcium. The soccer season that I first felt inspired to help this family I did something so simple – I asked coaches and parents to bring items to put into travel bags for Brooke and Katie as they were going to Texas to seek medical attention for Steve. We succeeded in making Leslie cry because of the gratitude that she felt and in letting this family know our thoughts traveled with them.

Brooke and my daughter Gracie are the same age, with Gracie being 7 days older. Each year when birthday parties were planned I would coordinate with Leslie on dates and times so we could celebrate each girl without conflict. As years passed, Brooke migrated toward band and focused on her academics, both of which she excelled at. Gracie chose to run cross country and pursue theatre, enjoying her own successes. Because our town was so small, I would still run into Steve and Leslie at the high school football games as they watched the band. We still extended social invitations to one another for cookouts and Super Bowl parties. And all the while I watched Steve's health further decline and the toll being a caregiver was taking on Leslie.

Through it all, whenever I would ask how it was going, or how they were feeling, both would respond "We're doing ok." If I said, "I don't know how you do it," Leslie in particular would say, "We just do what we need to do."

The pivotal moment in this story came without fanfare, with no crowds around us. The only people present were Leslie, me, Gracie, and in the distance a cashier. Gracie and I were leaving the local Rite-Aid and we ran into Leslie. It was in early January 2017 and I greeted Leslie with an ordinary "How are you and Steve?" She responded, "We're tired." That was it. Two words that profoundly impacted me. Why? Because I had never heard Leslie admit to being tired. Her "We just do what we need to do" was now more honestly expressed as "We're tired." One look at her and I knew that something was different.

The armor which Steve and Leslie had so gallantly carried for years had a crack in it. The wall which they had built was now foundationally shaking. They had hit a dark place and needed some light. Realizing this, I was called to action. I took the small openings as doors and I pushed my way through.

I started by reaching out with a week's worth of meals. Yes, not just one night, but a week's worth. Leslie was recovering from surgery, so I knew being on her feet wasn't good. On a Sunday afternoon I, and my then fiancé Victor, cooked up a storm. We prepared enough food for Steve and Leslie and extra for my family and for Victor. When we delivered the food, it was with the message "If you will wash these containers, we'll come pick them up on Friday and bring you more food for next week."

The next Sunday morning in church we learned that the pastor's wife was sick with a relapse of the flu. Knowing that we would be cooking anyway, we made a meal for the family and delivered it that same afternoon along with another week's worth of food to Steve and Leslie. It was later that same evening that the real fun began.

When Victor and I delivered that first round of food, we visited for a few minutes with Steve and Leslie. She was sitting in a recliner that was quite literally falling apart. The back had come loose and was leaning to one side. In Leslie's typically positive attitude she said, "This is the only place where I feel comfortable to sit because there isn't as much pressure on my back." She had created a makeshift work area using a lap tray so she could work on her laptop from that lopsided chair. The couch in their home had belonged to Leslie's grandmother. Steve's chair had also seen many better days. I am not telling you this with any judgment. With the family's medical issues and associated bills, they had to prioritize where their money went. For me their living room spoke of sacrifices made. Steve and Leslie had so many other burdens to bear. This was the opportunity I was looking for.

On the second Sunday of delivering food, I had a plan ready to put into place. I had called Brooke who was at college, asking for input to make sure I was on the right track. She became my first co-conspirator. It was a good thing she was away at college. As close as she is to her parents, I don't think she could have kept our secret otherwise. We didn't tell Katie until a little later because she still lived at home. We needed to be clandestine.

I told Victor who jumped on board. Together he and I went over to the home of Steve's brother and sister-in-law, John and Kris. I shared with them the plan I had in mind and solicited their help. Kris went into the bedroom and came out with cash money, becoming the first contributor to what was now an official mission. Together we made a list of people and groups that we could reach out to, each taking an assignment.

My contribution was to write a letter which was ultimately mailed, emailed, faxed or hand-delivered to an abundance of people. The challenge was to do this without Steve and Leslie knowing, while at the same time protecting their privacy and doing so in a respectful way. Steve and Leslie are stoic, very private people. They would NEVER ask for help. I was brazen and motivated enough to not wait for a request for help. I took a risk, but I knew my intentions were good. And besides, when the ball got rolling, I could share the blame with John, Kris and Brooke if any offense was taken. Ha!

I am going to share with you an excerpt from the letter I drafted that was circulated. It was tweaked depending on who the intended recipient was, but the bottom line message was the same. It outlined the three things we hoped to be able to gift to Steve and Leslie. My initial goal was furniture, but soon I set the stakes higher.

"In talking to family members, I have identified 3 of the biggest needs for Steve and Leslie. Steve is in desperate need of some significant dental surgery. The ultimate outcome would give him the ability to eat regularly again, which will improve his health and restore some of his dignity. The couple also needs new living room furniture, including a lift recliner. Their furniture is quite literally broken and falling apart. And thirdly, the family needs a break from the costs of daily items like food."

This description was followed in each letter by a specific request for funds, again depending on who the target recipients were. To select friends, members of my own church, and others in our local community who knew the family, particularly Band Boosters, I wrote: *"Here is my request ... realizing that I am asking boldly but knowing that God has laid this on my heart ... I am asking 75 people to each give $100 to aid this very deserving and needy couple."* Near the end of the letter I went on to state: *"More than anything I want them to know that they are not alone in their struggles, that others see or hear what they are going through, and that they experience God's love in the process."*

I won't list here all the places that we sent letters or made calls. But the responses received came from many different places. Churches, who only knew me and trusted my request, donated. Individuals donated. I reached out to my local dentist, someone that I certainly don't know personally and that I only see every six months. He is always attentive, taking the time to sit and look me in the eye as he provides care. I faxed over a letter to him on a Monday. The next morning, I was sitting in a meeting and my cell phone rang. I stepped out to take the call. It was my dentist's assistant, Glynnis. She told me Dr. Budde wanted Steve and Leslie to come in for a consultation so he could determine how he might help. I walked back into my meeting crying.

Shining a Light

I set an aggressive timeline for this plan, partly because I knew the need was great. This was verified when Steve posted the following on his Facebook page on the evening of February 25: *"Through our lives we all face dark moments in time, but no matter how dark it gets, we can always crack the door and let some light in."* Reading this, I smiled, knowing that in less than 24 hours so many others and I would be a part of bringing some light to this family.

Steve and Leslie were in a dark place and I wanted to share light with them, and the sooner the better. The campaign lasted two weeks. I would love to say that we raised the $7,500 that I had requested. We did not. But we were able to gift them with enough money, discounts and gifts in kind to touch all three categories of need.

The biggest gift of all to Steve and Leslie, and the one by which I am most humbled, was their reaction. On the afternoon of Sunday, February 26, a small group of family and friends gathered in the parking lot of the park near my home. I had texted Leslie and asked her if I could come by with one more gift. I texted because I was sure I couldn't speak to her on the phone without giving something away. Since my previous pattern was to deliver food on Sunday afternoon, I hoped she was expecting more of the same. I know they were expecting only Victor and me to show up.

That morning I had gone to Cincinnati to pick up Brooke, so she was present. Katie was at home and going into work later in order to participate. When I walked into the house, alone, Katie had to step into the hallway to hide her smile from her parents. A convoy was parked down the street, out of sight. I asked Leslie and Steve if they minded if more people came in. Leslie replied with a drawn out

"Oooookay." Steve was in his wheelchair, having a bad day physically and unable to stand. I stepped outside and gave the signal to those waiting.

One by one, family members and friends crowded into that small living room. Leslie's reaction was priceless as she began to question what was going on. "Hey, there's (name)!" and "Brooke! How did she get up here?" A high school buddy was there, leading to questions of how Mike got involved. By the time more than a dozen people were all inside, the tears were already flowing. And I will confess, as I type this part of the story I am doing so with tears flowing down my own face, humbled again by the memory of what transpired that afternoon.

I was the spokeswoman for the group. I started my speech by saying exactly what I shared above. This is not an I story or effort; it is a WE story about a group of people who cared enough to band together to help this struggling family. I am witness to the fact that the sense of community and love we all shared in those moments was palatable.

As I shared with Steve and Leslie what we had done, I handed Leslie a box of tissues early on as I knew she would need them. I ratted out their daughters for being conspirators and keeping secrets. I threw John under the bus by admitting that he had taken to Facebook to reach out to others. John never uses Facebook. When I announced that Steve would have a dental consultation, that Jack was holding money so that the couple could go pick out furniture, and when I handed them an envelope full of monetary contributions, I witnessed a miracle best described later by Steve himself in a follow up post:

"... someone opened the door today and let a whole lot of light in. It's easy to forget that you are loved so much by so many when you are chronically ill and all the struggles and hardships that you place on others with it. While I am humbled and thankful beyond measure for what you all did, I am most grateful for the company. This is not the life I wanted, health wise, but you all make it much more bearable. Thanks for your time and your kindness. It is appreciated."

The Greatest Gift of All

Look at the phrase that reads, "I am most grateful for the company." Our gifts were important, but the gift of community was more meaningful. Steve and Leslie needed to be reminded that they are an important part of the community of friends and family gathered that day or who donated to the cause, whether named or anonymously. The sense of community I felt by being able to champion that cause was extraordinary. So much so that I kept a screen shot of Steve's posts because I had a feeling that one day this story would be retold. Ta-da.

Conversation Starter

Angi listens to her heart and helps feed the hungry. Shannon and a coalition of citizens gather regularly to lend their voices to a solution for the opioid crisis. Jack is Jack doing what Jack does best when he hears a distress call, asking, "Do you know if they need anything?" Strangers banded together to raise money for a family at risk of losing their hope. None of our stories are "I" stories, but they wouldn't be told if aware individuals didn't step up to begin the conversation.

Red Flags

I want to make one other comment related to the story of Steve and Leslie. If you feel the need to say, "I don't know how you do it!" to someone, that is a sign that you should do something for that person. And, if they respond, "We just do what we need to do," the translation usually means "I give it my all, but that doesn't mean I'm not tired, frustrated or at times isolated because of the burdens I carry." Be aware of those around you who may need help. Listen to what people are telling you, even if you must interpret the true meaning behind their words.

PS: In helping Steve and Leslie, I attempted to contact Ellen DeGeneres through the nomination process outlined on her show's website. Ellen, if you or your staff happen to read this, know that it's not too late. Steve and Leslie continue to struggle mightily. I would be a willing co-conspirator to surprise them. I can keep a secret.

Chapter 6 Reflection

"Let us therefore approach the throne of grace with boldness, so that we may receive mercy and find grace to help in time of need." Hebrews 4:16

Q1: I chose as the emphasis word for this chapter "Aware." What obstacles get in the way of our being aware of the needs of others?

Q2: What reasons have you used in the past to not help someone or volunteer? Describe a time when you volunteered to help with a project and found yourself blessed in the process.

Q3: The pivotal point for me in the story with Steve and Leslie was her admitting that she was tired when we talked in the store. What other, more subtle signals do people give when they need help or encouragement?

Q4: Why do you think Steve was so appreciative of the company he received on the day we gifted him? How can you bring light to someone who is isolated, lonely or struggling?

Space intentionally left blank for your own thoughts.

Space intentionally left blank for your own thoughts.

~ ~ ~

Focus of Chapter 7:

Do you remember the old sitcom *Cheers* where a male patron would walk into the bar and everyone would scream, "Norm!"? I have three places in my life where I experience that same welcoming atmosphere. People know my name and miss me when I am not there. I experience a great sense of community in each place. As you read my stories, reflect on your own experiences of feeling welcomed in a social setting.

~ ~ ~

Chapter 7: This Lady Walks into a Bar
Social

When was the last time you did something spontaneous and new? For me, it was going to a dive bar. Ok, I have been to dive bars before. More than I should admit here. I went for the first time to a particular dive bar – The Phone Booth.

The Phone Booth is a local institution, having been around since the 1950s. The first night I went, I thought from the outside it was unassuming. Inside the building needed updating. At least I think it did. Every seat was taken; the floor was packed with people standing, waiting for a seat to open, or dancing. Every pool table was being used and smokers were standing outside braving the cold air to feed their habits. The place was hoppin'!

My Favorite Hangout

My night began in a much different setting, at a high-end wine store called Rumbleseat. On Friday nights the proprietors, Chris and Urmila, bring in bands to play live music. The bands rotate but on the same pattern. So, the same band plays on the first Friday, another on the second Friday, etc. There is no cover charge. You can bring in your own food. You can go and spend nothing at all, or you can drop 20 bucks on a bottle of wine. I L-O-V-E going there on Friday nights, especially the first Friday night when my favorite band – known locally as *Spill the Wine* – plays. November and December 2017 were particularly fun evenings. People were laughing and singing along. *Spill the Wine* plays music like Carly Simon's *You're So Vain* and

Janis Joplin's *Me and Bobby McGee* and other songs from the same era/genre. We all know every word to every song and we join in accordingly.

I like going on the first Friday because so many regulars do the same. It doesn't take long to realize the sense of community that has been established among those who gather. I am to the point where I am very comfortable going table to table, chatting with Donna or Carol or countless others. One guy comes and even though I have been told his name I still secretly refer to him as the Mayor. He enters alone, picks his spot to stand and people just come up to him all night long to talk.

On Friday night, January 5, 2018, things were different. Friends and I usually get to Rumbleseat early, around 5:45 at the latest. The band comes on at 7:00 but the place will be packed by 6:15. As we entered, Chris told us that the lead guitar player for *Spill the Wine*, Larry, was gravely ill. His wife, Toni, the lead singer, was with him. Most of the other regulars must have heard this beforehand because all night the place was mostly deserted. The keyboardist and other guitar player performed as a duo, but their songs were low key and reflected the mood that hung over the place.

The other thing that made this night different was that at 7:15 I received a voicemail message from Dan in Oklahoma telling me of Lewis' passing. I was in a place that felt like a preliminary wake, mourning the loss of my father-figure. Not exactly the fun-loving, carefree night I had experienced just one month prior. But for me, given the circumstances, it was somehow fitting.

Anyone who goes to Rumbleseat to listen to the bands

will tell you that they feel a sense of community. Why? In large part because of Urmila. She is a vibrant, vivacious Italian who not only knows about wine, but she remembers everyone's name, usually after only hearing it once. She greets everyone as if they are her closest friends. She has a beautiful, raspy voice and when she joins the band, it is show stopping. Chris and Urmila are the perfect pair when it comes to their business. He is low key, business-oriented and Urmila works the crowd.

The greatest testament to the community they have built among their regulars is the silent tribute Urmila paid to Larry and Toni. Usually she sings at least one or two songs with the band. On that January night, even though the duo encouraged her to take the lead, she didn't. She couldn't; she was too emotionally distraught over the illness of her close friend. We talked at length about that.

There was a woman sitting by herself at a nearby table. I went over and began to chat, introducing myself. It turned out that she was with the keyboard player but admitted that this was the first time she had come to Rumbleseat. She works nights and it is hard for her to attend many of her husband's (I am assuming they are married) gigs. But on this night, she had off so not only were they at Rumbleseat, but they were going to The Phone Booth afterwards. I admittedly had never even heard of the bar, only recently having moved to the same neighborhood. When I brought up the name back at my own table, everyone knew of The Phone Booth. Rumor had it that the place was soon closing temporarily due to a landlord/tenant dispute. The bar would be moving from its iconic location. If we were going to go, we needed to do it soon. Tom, Lucy, Diane and I went. I will admit doing so because I knew that as soon as I was home I would shed the impending tears for having lost Lewis. I was putting off the inevitable.

Mosey on Over

As I said, the Phone Booth was lively on this night. The band was in full force, with the lead singer playing a tambourine as he walked through the crowd, smiling at the women or punching the guys on the shoulder. Diane was ready to leave after about 5 minutes, but we made her stay.

It was obvious to me that the people gathered there felt their own sense of community in what undoubtedly was their favorite and regular hang out. At one point I moseyed back to where the pool tables were, taking a cursory look at the action. The Phone Booth is the kind of place where you mosey. A guy approached me and struck up a conversation. He stuck out his hand and gave mine a firm shake. "I'm Joe; do I know your name?" "Nope, I'm Sandra," I heartedly responded back. I liked Joe's style immediately. We talked small talk, and as I walked away, I had the impression that Joe was the Mayor of The Phone Booth.

We didn't stay long, maybe 30 minutes. The keyboard player and wife from Rumbleseat showed up, so I moseyed over their way to greet them. Tom almost got into a fight when he bumped some guy's chair. Tom later said that he could've taken the guy, but we didn't wait to find out.

In thinking about these two different places, I concluded that even though the clientele may be different, the goal is the same – to provide a place where people want to hang out in a neighborhood-like setting and feel as if they are part of a community. I feel that way about Rumbleseat and even though Diane may not tag along, I would go back to The Phone Booth in its new location and stay awhile.

More Than a Game

As I have mentioned, I belong to a Euchre card club. We play on Wednesday nights at Mack's Tavern with a rotating group of 40 – 50 people. The organizers are Rod and Pam. If there is an odd number of people present and not enough for a full table of four, Rod and/or Pam will sit out and not play, bouncing table to table chatting with folks between hands or subbing in when someone needs another drink or trip to the restroom.

One night I was chatting with Rod and he said, "Pam and I don't really care about playing cards. This was just a way for us to meet new people." I can tell you from personal experience that meeting new people is only a part of what is occurring around those hands of cards. We have come to celebrate with one another over birthdays or holidays. Invitations are made for other activities, such as local sporting events or Lenten fish fries. When someone is gone for a week or two, people will inevitably say, "I didn't see you last week." That always makes me feel good. We aren't just playing cards. We are building community.

It Can Happen Anywhere

I have just described to you three bars where I have witnessed community building in action. Community happens in many different places. It happens in a church in a small town on the first and third Tuesdays as volunteers pack food for kids. It happens in a comedy club which opens its doors for storytelling. It happens in Rite Aid as we greet our neighbors. Community happens in our homes when we invite friends over. It happens on our streets as we learn more about the people we live next to. And yes, it can happen in bars as well. The key is to recognize community for what it is and participate in building it. Even if it means doing something spontaneously, like walking into a bar.

Chapter 7 Reflection

"But the fruit of the Spirit is love, joy, peace, longsuffering, kindness, goodness, faithfulness, gentleness, self-control. Against such there is no law." Galatians 5:22-23

Q1: If I were to ask you where you experience a sense of community, what is the first place that comes to mind? Why?

Q2: When you experience a sense of community, how do you feel? Can you think of ways you can help others also experience a sense of community in the place you identified?

Q3: When was the last time you did something spontaneously? Did you enjoy the experience? Did you feel uncomfortable or like an outsider, or did you assimilate quickly? What helped you overcome any initial doubts about your choice?

Space intentionally left blank for your own thoughts.

Space intentionally left blank for your own thoughts.

~ ~ ~

Focus of Chapter 8:

It was important for me to add a chapter in this book about building community within our families because that is an area where I have struggled. My family of origin is not close, geographically or emotionally. It's not easy to admit that or to find ways to fill voids that have developed over many years. You might call this the "samsonite chapter," knowing that we all carry baggage with us throughout our lives. I invite you to consider ways to unpack that baggage to allow room for future blessings.

~ ~ ~

Chapter 8: Serenity

Accepting

Before I began writing the first draft of this chapter, I took a break. I had just written Chapter 6 which was a rather intense process. Several times during that chapter I had to walk away from my laptop because the emotions were so intense. I didn't want "ME" to get in the way of what was being created, if that makes any sense. I ate lunch as it was almost 3:00 and I was starving. I retrieved some laundry from the basement. I did two sinks full of dishes that had piled up. Before KJ moved out I was always a little miffed when he left dirty dishes in the sink for me to wash. At least this time they were all mine.

As I washed dishes, I looked out the window at my backyard. It had been snowing all day and probably 8 inches covered the underlying grass. I knew that days like this, when I could isolate myself in the house and focus solely on writing, would not come frequently. It was then that I knew I needed to use that time to bypass Chapter 7 for which I had a pretty good outline and tackle what I suspected would be the hardest chapter of all … this one.

All through the weekend I had been mindful of saying to God, "Allow me to be your instrument." This time I literally got on my knees and prayed something like this, "God, I need you to help me not get in the way here. I have a feeling that you are going to ask me to walk through some doors that I may not want to walk through. I also know some people may find their own healing through this journey, including me. For that reason, let's go."

I am including a chapter in this book on establishing a sense of community within family knowing that I am not an expert by any means on this topic. I have already mentioned that I have been divorced twice, I have been engaged two other times, and when I was a junior in college I gave a child up for adoption. Let me give you a bigger picture as to why I am not an expert on close family relationships.

Searching for Understanding

When I was 24 years old I took custody of my younger half-sister who was not quite 16. She was living with our mother in Oklahoma and I was in Nashville, TN. She lived with me for about 2 years, finished high school, and then moved back to Oklahoma. She came to live with me in Nashville because of some dynamics between her and our mother which caused Amy to run away from home. I interceded at that point. I won't speak here about the dynamics at play; I wasn't involved or present, so I can't bear witness. That part of the story is not mine to tell.

Within a month of Amy moving back, she was pregnant by the boyfriend with whom she had initially run away. It was one of those times when I really needed help sorting through my emotions and understanding the dynamics of my family of origin. I had invested a lot of energy in trying to help Amy get to a better place. I was hurt, angry and in many ways confused. In some ways my three siblings and I were alike. We all had made relationship choices that for three of us had led to what used to be called pregnancies "out of wedlock." The only reason my oldest sister hadn't gotten pregnant was because she was unable to have children. In other ways, my siblings and I were very different, at least from my perspective. I had moved away and was building my life. The attempt to help Amy had drawn me back into family dysfunction. I needed help in understanding my array of emotions. To do this, I sought professional counseling.

During one of my first appointments, the counselor, whose name I really wish I could remember because I would give him credit here, had me draw a genogram. If you research this term you will find that a genogram *"is a graphic representation of a family tree that displays detailed data on relationships among individuals. It goes beyond a traditional family tree by allowing the user to analyze hereditary patterns and psychological factors that punctuate relationships."* (www.genopro.com/genogram)

My genogram included six circles, one each for father of origin, mother, two sisters, a half-sister, and myself. There was also a square for my stepfather, Julius. The next step in creating the diagram was to draw lines between each adult and each child to represent how I thought each person related.

(DISCLAIMER: Do you watch the show *This Is Us*? On Tuesday, January 9, 2018 an episode aired showing Kevin in counseling for an addiction. One day of his residential treatment was set aside for family counseling. Spouses and Kate's fiancé were asked to leave, so that only members of the family of origin were present with a counselor. Technically, Randall had a different family of origin and was adopted, but don't hold me to technicalities here. Each character, including the mom, Rebecca, had a different perception of the family's history. Each sibling was carrying baggage rooted in their childhood. Same family, same home, same upbringing, but each with their own perceptions. Similarly, what I am about to share is MY perception of how family members related based on MY genogram as drawn by ME. If one of my sisters were asked, they would more than likely respond differently. Understood? Ok. Back to the lines on my genogram.)

The Cast of Characters

My father of origin was always closest to my sister Sharon, so I drew a direct line between the two. I haven't used his name in years, so perhaps you will indulge me when I refer to him using the acronym FoO instead of his legal name. FoO was a drunken SOB who beat the hell out of my mother on many occasions. I have two memories of him from childhood which are unsettling.

My mother had seemingly been closest to my sister Cathy, so a line connected them on my chart. In my perception, it was almost as if early on the two adults had taken sides.

Julius was Amy's biological father. He was a good Christian man, had a beautiful tenor voice and was good to our family, but it was only natural that he would favor his own daughter. Those two shapes were connected.

My circle was off to the side, not connected to any parental figure. Visually, this represented how I had always felt, which was a bit left out, as if I didn't belong in the family unit. It was at this point that the counselor invited me to add a square on the genogram to represent Lewis and Frances. (See Chapter 1 for reference.) In Lewis' obituary I am listed just after son Bob and daughter Myrna. I am listed as "adopted daughter Sandra." While I know that this is a sensitive subject for my family of origin, even in 1991 it was evident Lewis and Frances deserved a square on my chart.

Let me elaborate on comments made above to give you examples of why I felt left out. I share these not looking for any pity or to point blame at anyone. When I said earlier that I suspected God would have me walk through a few doors that I had closed previously, this is where the walking begins.

Childhood Memories

I said I have two vivid memories of FoO. One is of a night when he and my mother, whose name is Mary by the way, had gone to a party. She had made a ham to take, but when they came home she was carrying the uneaten ham. FoO was drunk and angry about something, telling her the ham was garbage and not fit to be eaten. I was in bed. From where my head laid I could see down the hallway into the living room. I couldn't see my mother, but I heard FoO's expletives and I saw the things he was throwing and smashing. And I heard my mother crying. The violent outburst lasted several minutes I suppose, with me lying there witnessing half of the crime scene. When the violence had passed, what happened next in the calm was telling. FoO got Sharon out of bed. He sat with her in a chair and read her a book, as if he were a good parent nurturing his child. Cathy got up and helped my mother, who was quietly holding back sobs and bruised, clean up the shattered glass and ceramic. And I laid in bed, watching it all from afar. Why didn't anyone come and get me? I suppose I should have been grateful to escape the chaos, but I wasn't. I was sad; I was alone. I was literally a spectator to this event happening just down the hall.

The other childhood memory I have is incomplete, probably due to a self-defense mechanism. I remember lying in my parents' bed with FoO in the middle of the day. I was maybe 4 years old. I remember acting like I was sleeping. I know this because FoO asked me at one point, "Are you asleep?" to which I quickly replied "Yes." I remember my mom opening the door, calling me out and saying, "That's enough." Enough what? While I don't remember any other specific details, I know that it is odd that I would have that memory. I know that there is an underlying negativity when I allow the bits of memory to surface. And I know that it wasn't long afterwards that my mother got the courage to divorce FoO. Within a year she married Julius.

I remember reading an article in a Cincinnati paper around 2003 or 2004 about a lady who had something like 15 children. When asked if she ever found herself loving one more than the others she said, "Sure, I love the one more who needs me the most at the time. That's when they need more loving."

I think that quote relates to my mother's relationship with Sharon and Cathy during my teenage years, as I perceived it. They both made life-altering choices at young ages and needed extra loving as a result. When I was in 8th grade my family moved from one side of Oklahoma to the other where Julius' twin brother lived. It was an odd time to move for my older sisters as they were a junior and sophomore in high school. Sharon had already been sneaking out of the house to be with boyfriends and on one occasion even ran away for several days. My mother knew that if Sharon was forced to move she would just run away again, so she allowed Sharon to marry as an underaged minor. The ceremony was held before we left.

Cathy became a mother at the age of 16, by just a few weeks. She turned 16 and then her daughter was born a month later. I remember early in the pregnancy she had a hard time being able to tell our mom and Julius. She was extra clingy and would sit on our mom's lap. When she finally broke the news, it was hard on everyone. Rightfully so, our mom spent a lot of time with Cathy; she needed it. I don't begrudge that for a minute. This is just a piece of the puzzle that makes up my formative years.

I mentioned earlier that Julius had a beautiful tenor voice. He was part of a gospel quartet that traveled every weekend to what we simply called "singings." His brother Joel sang bass. Sometimes I went along, sometimes I didn't. Amy inherited her dad's musical talent. That girl has a voice that you could sit and listen to for hours. If she is a song bird, then her four daughters are her backup canaries. Assuming that canaries are pretty to listen to. Maybe whippoorwills?

Putting the Puzzle Together

The counselor used my genogram as a tool to discuss family dynamics. What was so profound to me was his ability to understand and describe the traits of family members without ever having met them.

When I described how close FoO and Sharon were, the counselor said, "Let me describe Sharon to you." He said she probably had a hard time maintaining relationships and probably veered towards destructive relationships due to the unhealthy connection between her and FoO. Sharon was married multiple times and had multiple other relationships, most if not all of which were abusive. One time a guy threw her so hard against a stove that she blacked out and lost partial hearing. She was the only one of us siblings who remained in contact with FoO over the years. I tried to reach out to him once in college. A receptionist had answered and told him his daughter was on the line. When he realized it was me and not Sharon, he hung up. I guess this makes three memories I have.

I don't remember exactly what the counselor said about Cathy and Amy, but I remember being blown away by the fact that he described each one to a tee. The thing that was most helpful was that he helped me understand that my feelings, my emotions were normal based on the family history. Hearing that I was normal or that what I was feeling could be explained was well worth the money paid.

Ongoing Conversation

This would not be the last time I would seek counseling as an adult. I mentioned in the Introduction that I attended counseling with Barbara after my second divorce. One of my favorite catch phrases is "It's all good." Whenever I would say this to Barbara she would reply, "No it's not. If it was all good, you wouldn't be paying me." Now with my friends I often jokingly say "It's all good, Barbara."

When I describe my relationship with my mother to others I often say something like, "We don't have a warm fuzzy relationship," or "There are many reasons why my family is in Oklahoma and I am in Ohio," either of which are usually followed by, "but, it's all good." Some people nod in understanding. For others this is hard to comprehend. I will admit that at times it is hard for me to comprehend, even if I have the benefit of rounds of counseling to try and understand it all.

I have not lived in Oklahoma since I graduated college. Separation can be a healthy move if it allows us to distance ourselves from unhealthy or dysfunctional settings. Sometimes it can also be a defense mechanism, helping to put distance between ourselves and pain. I suppose my distant relationship with my mother and my siblings is a bit of both. I could write story after story of times when I did this, or they did that. We all have assumed roles characteristic of dysfunctional families.

I don't know that I can adequately put into words how this has played out in our adult lives. Again, I can only speak from my own experience. I haven't seen Cathy in several years and then only once in the past 15 or so. We don't call each other. I don't even think that I have her phone number. Periodically I see things about her life on social media, but only through posts by other family members. The same is true of my relationship with Amy, but we have seen each other more often. Because of our earlier closeness, she tends to be the buffer for me when I am back in Oklahoma. But we aren't close either.

My relationship with my mother continues to be distant. There have been many times that I have wanted to broach ways to connect with her. Part of the problem is that my family never talked about the issues that divided us. I offer the story about my FoO and my memory of being in that room with him as one example. I have no idea what memories Cathy has from being in a house with FoO. I have no idea what memories Amy has of the time surrounding the death of Julius and our mother's reaction which led to her being hospitalized. My mother and I have never talked about my taking custody of Amy. We just never talked about such things. Today we don't talk about anything. If you can't talk about the little things, it is impossible to talk about the big things.

Another problem, which I readily identify, is that family members often need what others cannot give. Parents can only love the way they have been taught to love. I have always wanted my mother to tell me she was proud of my accomplishments. Just because she doesn't verbalize it, doesn't mean she isn't proud of me. It's just hard to know that she is. In a small group one time I heard this described as "loved but not validated."

I wish I had a happy ending to the story of my family of origin. I can't say there is because the ending has yet to be written. As you read the postscript to this chapter you will see there is a ray of hope.

Faith and a Better Understanding

I have a plaque hanging in my home which reads, "Faith makes things possible, not easy." The one thing that my mother, sisters and I do have in common is our strong faith. We are all actively involved in faith communities that, from my experience, provide a great means of hope. I also put a high value on the power of prayer. Every word typed in this book has been backed up with prayer. I will reflect more on the power of faith later in this chapter.

I said upfront that I am not an expert on close family relationships. Maybe you now have a glimpse as to why I say that. But let me suggest this: maybe I am an expert on understanding the need for building community within our families. Understanding the need and knowing how to meet that need are often two different things.

While editing this book, I began attending meetings for Adult Children of Alcoholics ("ACA"). The definition of an Adult Child has been helpful to me. I have learned that adults carry with them the coping mechanisms they learned as children, often assuming similar roles. As a child, I felt like I was an outsider looking in at my family. As an adult, I became an overachiever, looking for some recognition. I became independent and organized and a planner, attempting to take control as much as I could. I carried these traits into my relationships. This is especially impactful of my second marriage.

My first marriage consisted of what I now understand to be a typical ACA scenario. I hooked up with someone that I thought I could fix. It only took me four years to realize that I couldn't. I am not going to give a lot of space to that relationship in this book, even knowing it is one of those life stories that make me who I am today. I say this knowing that the by-products of that marriage are my two children, whom I love dearly. For that reason, even with all the hardships of a failed marriage, I wouldn't change a minute if it meant not having my son and daughter.

Role Play

I entered into marriage with my second husband Dave with both of us having come out of extremely dysfunctional first marriages. Dave was divorced for six years and I for ten. Our marriage lasted for 7.5 years. We joked that we had a twisted Brady Bunch thing going on as he had four boys and I had my two children. The failing housing market of 2008 curtailed our plans to sell two houses and move into one large enough for our blending family. Instead we crammed together into my three-bedroom house and became landlords renting his. As the months and years went on, I thought that if I could do everything for everyone then the combined family would work. My need to control chaos and make everything alright or perfect shifted into high gear. Aside from the fact that this feat is impossible, it thwarts the ability for others to lend their own voices and gifts to the creation of the family.

As I look back, I now realize that I took on another characteristic of an Adult Child. Perceived critique and criticism translated into "you're not good enough." While we were dating I went to a holiday meal with Dave's family, hosted by his mother. I had offered to bring desserts. I made two or three pies and a cake. When I arrived, I realized that Dave's mom had several desserts already on hand. She had cereal and marshmallow treats because one grandson liked those. She had a cheesecake sampler, because another grandson liked cheesecake. Guess which desserts were eaten and which weren't. Had Dave's mom suggested I make favored desserts I would have. Instead, my uneaten desserts left me feeling like an outsider.

When you join a family unit that has an established history, which is the case in all blending families, it is hard to assimilate. It is even harder when the two adults do not have the tools needed to create anything other than dysfunction. You settle into roles that are comfortable. In our case, Dave was passive and I was aggressive. I took on the roles of director, planner, organizer, over-achiever. On many occasions, my desire to do something beneficial for one of my stepsons was met with resentment by various family members. When my intentions were misunderstood, this translated into "you're not good enough" in my mind.

I also assumed the role of spectator. I would plan perfectly-detailed gatherings, and then sit on the edge of the room. If we hosted the gathering, I would sit in the adjoining kitchen listening to stories being retold of events in which I had not participated. If the gathering was at my mother-in-law's, I would often leave early under the pretext of giving Dave time alone with the boys. In reality, I was escaping the feeling of being an outsider and not belonging. I wanted to be on the inside, but I didn't know how.

Dave and I did not know how to communicate effectively. I had assumed so many roles that there was little room for collaboration. Barbara once asked me what would happen if I just let certain things play out, without feeling the need to jump in and take control. I don't remember what my verbal response was. I do recall a feeling of despair. I simply didn't know how to step back. And if I did, would I become even more of a spectator?

Lessons Learned

Writing this book and particularly this chapter has provided me the opportunity for realistic reflection. One trait that I have for which I am grateful is that of optimism. Much of this stems from the firm faith foundation that my mother, Julius, Lewis and Frances instilled in me as I was growing up. In my family, if you were well enough to sit up in bed on Sunday morning you were well enough to go to church. In church, I always felt that I belonged. I heard countless sermons on hope and love and forgiveness. Those lessons serve me well as I reflect on what needs to happen to build real community in our families.

First, I think we must be willing to forgive and understand that we all come to the playing field of life carrying with us the skills we learned as children. I am reminded of a 2013 Volkswagen commercial where a dad is teaching his son to throw a baseball. Viewers first see the son throwing with an awkward, almost painful motion. We then see the father move to pick up the ball and throw it back, using the same awkward motion. We realize that the son is only mimicking his dad. Children coming from dysfunctional families do the same thing. Our parents can only teach us what they know. Perhaps one thing that saves us in the end is an understanding that we may need coaching to throw the ball differently. We must be willing to allow coaches to intercede and right a few wrongs. Coaches are counselors, healthy personal support systems, or support groups. Just as athletes get better with practice, so do families trying to break the cycle of dysfunction.

Secondly, I think we must be willing to cut ourselves some slack. We can look back, do repeated V8 face palms and say, "I should have (fill in the blank)." Or, we can try and make amends where we can, wear a few emotional bandages, and move forward stronger with hope and love. We can't beat ourselves up because our families are not perfect. All we can do is give our best.

For me, another healthy step has been to take to heart the ACA version of the Serenity Prayer as taken from the newcomer's booklet: *"God, grant me the serenity to accept the people I cannot change, the courage to change the one I can, and the wisdom to know that one is me."* There are many reasons why I live in Ohio, away from my family in Oklahoma. I cannot change my FoO; even if I could he passed away almost 25 years ago. I cannot change my mother or former spouses or anyone else. It takes enough effort just to focus on what I need to change in myself.

When we reach the point of being able to forgive, of accepting others for who they are, then and only then can we build real community within our families. We must quit beating ourselves up for past mistakes and begin focusing on self-improvement. Then and only then will we find serenity. And that is the hope I am clinging to and the prayer I continue to lift.

PS: I reference several times in this book a number of what I call "God moments." I picture God in heaven, with a conductor's baton, orchestrating a series of events that I could never have composed.

I struggled writing this chapter, striving to balance the candidness of my own story with respect for stories not mine to tell. I also struggled with the timing of when to talk to my mother about the past. I don't want all the answers to questions not asked. I simply want to understand the present to get to a better future.

At a pivotal point in my editing the book, God orchestrated the first of those conversations. I won't go into all the details here, but in that conversation my mother and I talked about the different ways that people show love. There was humor, there was insight, there were confessions; steps were taken toward better understanding. It was a perfect example of what I hope my stories can accomplish. It was, in short, quite a moment.

Chapter 8 Reflection

"I know how to be abased, and I know how to abound. Everywhere and in all things I have learned both to be full and to be hungry, both to abound and to suffer need. I can do all things through Christ who strengthens me."
Philippians 4:12-13

Q1: What parts of Chapter 8 resonated strongly with you? Why?

Q2: Read the ACA Serenity Prayer through several times, focusing on each of the three sections. What other verses or words of wisdom do you carry in your heart and mind that you have found to be empowering?

Q3: Psalm 46:10 reads in part, "Be still and know that I am God." Waiting for family relationships to improve is hard to do. We are a society of instant gratification. What relationship are you focused on where you may need to be still and know that God is in control?

Space intentionally left blank for your own thoughts.

Space intentionally left blank for your own thoughts.

~ ~ ~

Focus of Chapter 9:

In our attempts to build community, we often must overcome challenges or barriers that hinder meaningful relationships. In this chapter, I share with you one of my barriers. I invite you to consider your own. And, at the end of this chapter, you will learn the meaning behind the daffodils. Not going to lie, it's a pretty cool story.

~ ~ ~

Chapter 9: Recycle Bin

Motivated

Three and a half bottles of wine. One bottle of champagne leftover from New Year's Eve. One bottle of Prosecco on hand to make Mimosas for girlfriends. Two cans of beer.

Ten minutes before writing this chapter that is what I poured down the drain in my kitchen sink. I took a Trader Joe's paper bag and filled it with the now empty bottles and cans. I opened the door in my kitchen and stepped out onto my small patio. I tossed the bag of glass and aluminum into my recycle bin. I then sat down to write this chapter which is an addition to the original manuscript.

A Growing Conviction

Knowing how much I enjoy going out with friends and meeting new people over cards or while listening to music, for a year or more I have been convicted by the amount of alcohol that I drink. I first remember wondering if I had a problem around the beginning of Lent in 2017. In the Christian calendar, Lent begins on Ash Wednesday and ends on Good Friday, just before Easter. Some Christians use this time to give up something which to them symbolizes temptation. It might be chocolate or desserts. Some people take the opposite approach, choosing to intentionally do something good for others throughout the holy season. Over the years I have not been very successful in following through on my Lenten commitments, although I do find myself thinking about the options. You might compare this to my making a New Year's resolution. I contemplate losing weight. I consider packing lunch more often and limiting my eating out to one day a week. Contemplating and committing are two different actions.

I remember thinking in 2017 that I should give up alcohol for Lent. I also remember the fear which came over me at the time. I couldn't put into words why I was fearful, so instead I joked about the option with my friends. Deep down the last thing in the world I wanted to give up was alcohol. The thought truly scared me. So, I gave up nothing at all.

One Saturday night in May, my then fiancé and I went to Columbus to watch a Columbus Crew soccer match. My son's birthday is May 5 and Victor's birthday is May 7. I had bought four tickets to the soccer game on May 6 for all of us to attend, along with KJ's girlfriend. That Saturday was cold and rainy. We waffled back and forth as to whether we should attend the game, none of us really wanting to be miserable in the open stadium. In the end, Victor and I went alone. On the drive home, we talked about ideas for our wedding reception which was planned for 14 months later. I told Victor that I had asked Urmila, the part owner of Rumbleseat mentioned in Chapter 7, to bartend at the reception. Victor got very quiet and withdrawn. He didn't want alcohol at our reception. He had past relationships where family and friends had real issues with alcohol. I became angry that he compared me to those people. I scoffed. How could we not serve alcohol to our guests? I honestly couldn't envision such a thing.

In June, I attended an estate auction. As I sat in the audience waiting for the items I wished to bid on, my phone rang. Gracie was crying and upset. She was embarrassed because she had been at a party the night before and blacked out from drinking too much alcohol. The party was at her apartment and she was protected by her roommates, so I wasn't worried about her safety. I didn't feel the need to scold her. Instead, I counseled her on the safer way to drink. I told her to eat beforehand, rather than waiting for the food at the party. I suggested she alternate water with her alcoholic drinks to stay hydrated. I encouraged her to not try and drink as much as her older friends who had more experience and a higher tolerance level. At one-point Gracie laughed and said, "Mom, you know you're teaching me how to drink?" I replied, "No, I'm teaching you how to remember everything that happens at a party." I joked with my friends that I probably lost a few nominations for Mother of the Year with that conversation.

In September, Victor and I had broken off our engagement and were attempting to navigate the now fading relationship. A few months earlier we had committed to attend the wedding of a co-worker of his, so I agreed to go along as his date for the evening. Because our relationship was strained, we both drank more than we should have. I got home around 11:00 and immediately went to bed. Ninety minutes later I was awakened by a phone call. A young lady told me she was with KJ and two of his military friends and that KJ had too much to drink. She said he was passed out in the street in front of our house. After I changed out of my pajamas and went outside, the young lady told me she had rung my doorbell several times. In my defense, I am a heavy sleeper on most given nights. Aided by alcohol, I had not heard the bell. I found my son, surrounded by his buddies, lying in his own vomit in the middle of the street. When we couldn't get him inside, I had someone call 911. Recent national news reports of college students dying from alcohol poisoning was a key factor in my decision. As the paramedics took him to the emergency room, I trailed behind in my own car. Later I would be told that several people had bought my son numerous drinks after he was past the point of being able to decline, thinking it was humorous to do so. I once again found myself having a parent/child conversation about how to drink safely when hanging with friends.

In the fall of 2017 I had a rediscovered freedom to go out with friends any time I wished. I wasn't tied to a dating relationship. I didn't have children at home dependent on me for rides or meals. It was not unusual for me to socialize 5 or 6 times a week, which meant I was drinking 5 or 6 nights a week.

At my rental house, I had the freedom to decorate it any way I wanted. I bought a small cabinet with glass doors to display my entertaining dishes. I decorated the top with bar pieces. I added small signs that read "If I ever go missing, I want my picture on a wine bottle instead of a milk carton. That way my friends will know I am missing." and "This wine is making me awesome."

The first Friday night in December, I went to Rumbleseat to listen to my favorite band. A friend and I shared three bottles of wine. We had drunk two when a male patron, who was buying drinks for his two female friends, bought us a bottle as well. Like KJ earlier in the summer, I had passed the point of declining. I remember driving home that night with the windows down and the radio blaring. I had learned over the years that if you yell loudly while driving it temporarily sharpens your senses. I remember staggering into my house and collapsing on the bed. Mostly I remember waking up around 3:00 a.m. and barely making it to the bathroom where I threw up multiple times. I thought I contained my retching by throwing up in the trash can, but the next morning I discovered vomit everywhere in the bathroom. I had to wash the shower curtain and scrub the walls and floor. KJ was still living with me at the time but had spent the night at his grandparents' house. That morning, I had to be at church to assist with the retirement reception for our senior pastor. How ironic that I did so with a hangover.

I didn't touch alcohol for a week after that episode. My stomach simply would not allow me to do so. The following weekend I was hosting a brunch for ten ladies. Several offered to bring alcohol. Initially, I declined, which was baffling to some. Rather than admit that I had a problem controlling my drinking, I used the excuse that someone at the party would not be comfortable if we served alcohol. In the end, I relented and served Mimosas. My abstinence was short lived.

The holiday season came and went. I found myself driving two other times when I know I should not have been. Each time as I awakened the next morning, I thanked God for his protection and vowed to do better the next time.

In February 2018 I hosted a dinner and book discussion

at my home. I once again offered wine and spritzers as beverages. Just after dinner, as we were moving into the living room for our discussion, a guest commented when she saw me pour a soft drink instead of white wine. I thought it odd that she would notice such a thing, unless my friends had started watching how much I was drinking. I again used humor to mask my true reaction.

Through all of this I convinced myself that I could socialize, drink and still be safe. I had safely driven home while highly intoxicated. I had survived nights of rooms spinning and vomit-covered floors and each time my rationalizations became easier to recite. The problem with that theory was that my drinking was not limited to social gatherings. I found myself one evening sitting in front of the TV, with a glass of wine, wondering when the last day was that I had not drunk alcohol. I honestly could not remember. All I knew was that more and more I was drinking, and my limits were being continually stretched beyond what was safe or healthy.

Not long after this revelation I had a biometric screening done at my office. My weight had ballooned to the obese category given my height. My body mass index was high. My cholesterol was high. When the nurse practitioner counseled me on my results, I made several excuses as to why I had such numbers. In the back of my mind I knew the biggest culprit was alcohol.

The Catalysts for Change

So how did I come to the point of pouring what was about a week's worth of alcohol and two bottles of champagne down the drain and throwing the remnants into a recycle bin? God spoke to me through a renewed acquaintance, a trusted friend and a movie.

Catalyst #1

Just after writing my first draft of this book, I called an old high school classmate who has 25 years of experience in publishing. Betsy agreed to help me by being an editor. She read the book before this chapter was added. I asked her, "Given that you knew me so well in high school and we lost touch, what in the book or about me now surprises you the most?" I honestly expected her to say the adoption story. Instead, she replied, "You talk a lot about alcohol." That simple response blew me away. While I understand that Betsy made her comment in comparison to the very straight-laced person she knew in high school, I was left wondering about the impression I give to others who are around me more often. I didn't like being immediately associated with alcohol and it caused me to ponder.

Catalyst #2

There are few people in this world that I trust more than my friend Dar. One Monday afternoon we were texting each other about shared plans later that evening. Without going into detail here about the context of our conversation, I sent her a text which in part read:

I am truly happier now than I have been in quite some time. Major strides made in that regard. I am truly content in the knowledge that some relationships don't work for various reasons.

Dar responded:

"I would be someone in your life that wouldn't confirm your contentment with where you are in your life journey."

Again, a one-line response from a trusted source caused me to stop and ponder. Even though I clarified with Dar what I meant, which had nothing to do with overall contentment, I did wonder what, if anything, was keeping me from being truly content. My immediate thought was my struggle with alcohol.

Catalyst #3

The shared plan that Dar and I had that Monday was to go see the faith-based movie *I Can Only Imagine* along with Dar's husband Jim. What an inspiring movie! The story chronicles events leading up to the release of the song with the same title by MercyMe. Bart is the lead singer and main character. The movie takes the audience through his life as a child and young adult in a very dysfunctional family. The song, which was the band's first #1, was released after Bart reconciled with his abusive father and became more self-aware of the scars he was carrying. As I sat there in the darkened theatre, I watched the movie and recognized several parallels to my own life.

Location – Different events in the movie happen in Oklahoma City and Nashville, two cities that I have lived in previously.

Emotional barriers – Several times in the movie different people tell Bart that when he is engaging with others he pulls back and walls come up. Betsy said the same thing about my initial draft of this book.

Reconciliation – Bart was distanced both geographically and emotionally from his parents and needed to address that before he could truly be happy.

Sanctuary – In high school, Bart found sanctuary and guidance in church. He also had memorable experiences at church camp. I always loved going to Camp Egan in Tahlequah, Oklahoma and as a high school youth assumed every leadership role I could at church.

Support – Bart had several people around him who encouraged him; he had a support system in place of people who became like family to him. You'll see my parallel in the next chapter.

These collective factors caused me to become reflective and stirred something deep inside. In a moment, all the conviction that I had been fighting for a year or more came to the forefront and I could no longer ignore that I had a drinking problem.

That night, after seeing the movie, I went home and poured all the alcohol in my house down the drain. I then spent two hours and the ensuing week writing and thinking about why this needed to be done. This leads me to why this chapter is included in a book on building community.

Barriers to Authenticity

Alcohol or other crutches can become a barrier to building real, meaningful community with others. Hang with me here. I am not judging anyone or saying that drinking alcohol in moderation is wrong. The challenge I am facing is the ability to drink in moderation. When I am intoxicated or just plain drunk, I make poor choices. I don't want to substitute real, authentic joy for the happy, giddy, "no worries," or "it's all good" feeling that comes from drinking alcohol.

Drinking as much as I was isn't healthy. Alcohol affects my weight and my cholesterol. When I rely on alcohol in the evenings I am not productive. I found myself choosing between constructive activities such as taking a walk, writing, or even doing household chores and sitting on the couch with a good bottle of wine. I tried to categorize the latter as "relaxing."

I found myself grappling with what my reputation was becoming. More and more friends were gifting me with cards, pictures and trinkets that all had a wine theme. Granted, most of them were humorous and made me laugh. Because my friends didn't know that I was becoming more and more convicted by the problem I was trying to ignore, the gifts lost their luster.

Drinking alcohol led me to make poor financial choices. It was not uncommon for me to go out for the night and drop $40 on dinner and drinks. Multiply that times three or four times a week and I was living beyond my means. I am comfortably middle-class, but this pattern of excessive spending on alcohol created a financial roadblock to other dreams or goals I have for the future. The week that I poured the alcohol down the sink I went out four nights in a row. That Friday, I went back and added up my expenses. In total I spent $41, or the equivalent of one night of previous binging.

As I have noted in other chapters, building community requires several intentional actions including awareness and transparency. In looking back, I had become more and more aware of my dependency on alcohol. Because I was trying to hide it from my friends and even make light of it, I was not being honest or transparent with them or myself. For me, because I couldn't drink in moderation, I became fearful of what I was becoming. Fear, lack of awareness, and lack of transparency hinder community. And that is why I made the choice to recycle my dependency on alcohol and begin to create a more authentic me. I will still enjoy social gatherings. I will still walk into bars. I simply have to admit that I have limitations and focus on the end goal – a happier, healthier me; which in turn will lead to happier, healthier community with others.

PS: The Daffodil Story

Not quite 2 weeks after I poured the alcohol down my sink I was at home, doing chores and packing for a weekend trip. I was having a rough night. Not going to lie … I really wanted a beer. I could taste it without even opening a can. My mouth was dry and I longed for the familiar, comfortable feeling I could get from drinking. I told my home stereo to play MercyMe. Several songs came on and then *I Can Only Imagine* played. I told the stereo to repeat the song. As it played, I sat on the couch, holding my head in my hands. I was near tears. As the song ended, I turned around and was stopped in my tracks. On my kitchen table was a daffodil plant that Dar had brought to me three nights earlier. When she brought it, the plant had not yet bloomed. It was simply a pot of green stems. On this night, I had sat at the table eating dinner, just 30 minutes prior. The plant still had not bloomed. Now, as I turned around, the plant was in full bloom with yellow, floral cups opened wide. I had been sitting on my couch, in despair, missing the crutch that alcohol had become. When I turned around and saw the plant suddenly in bloom, I was reminded of God's grace and His ability to change the dormant into beautiful creations. I was reminded of how He could change me, if I would allow him. As Ann put in a text to me when I told her the story ... *"God is showing you JOY is coming and how much he loves you. He has you. Loves you as you are and will not forsake you. Trust and listen."* I can only imagine.

Chapter 9 Reflection

"Or do you not know that your body is the temple of the Holy Spirit who is in you, whom you have from God, and you are not your own? For you were bought at a price; therefore, glorify God in your body and in your spirit, which are God's." 1 Corinthians 6:19-20

"Therefore, if anyone is in Christ, he is a new creation; old things have passed away; behold, all things have become new." 2 Corinthians 5:17

Q1: Convictions have a way of gnawing at us until we are ready to respond. Describe a time when you felt convicted to do something.

Q2: Messages we need to hear come to us through friends, movies, and songs on the radio. Think of and describe a time when you were profoundly moved by something you heard or watched. Why do you think you were receptive to the message?

Q3: What was the last resolution you made and kept? What served as your motivation?

Q4: If you could sum up in just a few words what you want your reputation to be, what words would you use?

Space intentionally left blank for your own thoughts.

Space intentionally left blank for your own thoughts.

~ ~ ~

Focus of Chapter 10:

In our efforts to build community with others, it is essential to take a few moments and thank those for whom we are grateful. No one makes this journey through life alone. As you read my gratitude chapter, think of the people in your own network of support. Who do you need to thank today?

~ ~ ~

Chapter 10: Better Than a Sister
Grateful

If Chapter 8 was the hardest one to write in this book, Chapter 9 was a close second. This chapter however, was by far the easiest. Because here I get to give shout outs to the people who give me the greatest sense of community, the girlfriends who to me are better than sisters. Why? Because we didn't grow up together and argue about each other's clothes or the bathroom or secretly hide crushes like the one I had on Harold when he took Cathy to homecoming instead of me. And, frankly, as you learned previously, I am closer to these ladies than I am my own family. I firmly believe that we are given two families in this life – one that we are born into and one that we choose. I truly love the members of my chosen family.

In September 2015, I had probably the best Girls' Night Out event I have ever hosted on my back patio. Dave and I had separated for 6 months earlier in the year and had just gotten back together to try and make our marriage work. The purpose of the GNO was to thank the invited ladies for their support during those 6 months. Little did I know how much more I would need them in the months to come when Dave and I realized we couldn't make a go of it. I had also just run my first half marathon two weeks prior, so I was celebrating my success. All these ladies had proven to be valued cheerleaders.

At each place setting, I had a card addressed to one of the invitees, which in turn assigned seating. Even though I love all my friends, one or two of them get along better with some than others. It happens. The notes captured so perfectly my gratitude that I do not feel the need to recreate the wheel here. I will simply make an introduction and then reiterate my affection for each.

Karen, aka my Evil Twin. In early 2014 I had a horrible battle with pneumonia and was looking to get healthier. I was also in need of some stress relief given what was going on with my marriage. So, from about September 2014 through the summer of 2015 I participated in a Zumba class taught by the incomparable Debbie and Tammy. It was there that I met Karen. In class we were quite the pair, doing mostly "solos" in the back of the room as we moved to the music. Tammy dubbed us the evil twins. That's fine with me, but I'm the youngest. My note to her read:

Karen, I MISS YOU!!! Do you know what the best part of Zumba was for me? It wasn't the exercise or the music or the funny people that we could give nicknames to. It was the new friendships and the fact that I smiled just pulling into the parking lot, knowing laughter would soon follow. What most of you didn't realize was that, for some personal reasons, Zumba was a lifeline for me ... a time when I could release some pent-up stress and use exercise and laughter as cheap therapy. And, of course, I will never forget the divine providence of your helping me find a retirement home for my beloved Roscoe. Every time I go to Zumba, I still think something is missing because you aren't there. I am so very, very glad that our paths crossed. Tonight is about friendship and saying THANK YOU for all the support I have received over the past several months. You are the best Evil Twin EV-er!

Dar, aka my former hairstylist and the best Prayer Partner a girl could ever have. Talk about building a sense of community! Dar was and is an expert. As a hair stylist (she retired in December 2016), Dar knew the importance of making people feel welcomed. Doing hair was never just a business for her. It was simply a mechanism to build relationships. That's why so many of her clients wore sack cloth and ashes well into 2017. We celebrated with her in retirement but mourned the loss of community we all felt entering her shop. See my acknowledgements at the end of this book for one more note about Dar. My note to her read:

Dar, this past spring, as many things in my world were unraveling, you and I had lunch and you reminded me of Psalm 46:10 ... Be still and know that I am God. I cannot tell you how many times I have repeated this simple sentence over and over again, breathing in the assurance that not only was God on my side, but good friends were as well. Over the years you have been my #1 prayer partner; I simply know that if I ask you will be faithful in lifting me up in prayer. I cannot thank you enough for your perspective, your support, your words of wisdom and understanding and encouragement. You are a great friend and I love you dearly. With the utmost sincerity ... THANK YOU.

Ann, aka my Accountability Partner or "AP." When I had pneumonia in 2014 I first went to bed on Monday. I would stay there for two weeks. On Wednesday, Ann had a heart attack at work. We were just becoming friends as a job change for her meant more interaction between us. Over the two weeks of our individual bed rest, we texted each other daily. My first outing as my strength slowly returned, other than to the doctor, was to Ann's house. Neither one of us had the energy to do more than sit and talk, but I had an inkling, and maybe she did, too, that our bond was just beginning to form. Today, I can't imagine life without her friendship. My note to her read:

Ann, so, is it just me, or does it seem like we have known each other for a very long time? I guess we are just really good at packing numerous memories into the span of 18 months. It sounds crazy to say that I am grateful our two serious ailments occurred simultaneously last year. I thought then that you were a lifeline of sorts for me; someone I could text and commiserate with. Little did I know how much of a lifeline you would become. I cannot think of a single challenge, goal or significant event over the past year that I have tackled that you haven't been there to support me. I jokingly chastised you for thanking me so much for helping with Jenna's wedding. But I cannot possibly thank you enough for your friendship and support over the past several months. Here's hoping future memories are equally as numerous!

Mary, the friend who is most like an older sister whom I adore dearly but clash with most often. Mary is adventurous and loves to plan, which is usually where our clashes occur because so do I. She is great at nurturing friendships, always ready with an invitation to do something or go somewhere. She is social and outgoing and a great mix of being the corporate compliance officer (before she retired) who would send inappropriate emails to your office that would make you laugh hysterically. My note to her read:

Mary, when thinking of our friendship, I have thought often during recent years of how misleading first impressions can be. Little did I know some 11 or 12 years ago when you first interviewed with Bill what a joy it would be getting to know you. It has been so nice having a kindred spirit, someone who is always ready for an adventure and who makes those adventures all the more fun. I have so appreciated your thoughtfulness and presence over these past several months. Whether it was a simple lunch, a wine festival in NOLA, or a Reds game in sunny July, I have appreciated your friendship and the quiet manner in which you support me (and our Gracie).

Melodee – of all the people listed here Mel is the one that I see the least often these days. She is a workaholic and needs to find balance in her life. Said lovingly, but I am only repeating what she herself says. In any conversation with Melodee you will find yourself laughing so hard that you will simultaneously need a tissue for your tears and an adult diaper if you have bladder control issues. My note to her read:

Melodee, I will honestly not go to The Greene anytime soon without thinking of that hilarious time when we sat in a deluge of rain, eating our picnic and drinking our smuggled alcohol, as other, more slightly sane people sought shelter in permanent structures. When a person is going through a time of trial, sometimes it is those little, unexpected moments of laughter and adventure that help to brighten up the time. I have so appreciated hanging out with you, your continued humor and laughter, and your genuine frankness about life. I know that you too have been going through a hard few months; I only hope that I have repaid your kindness with my own.

Charlene – another friend that is sometimes hard to get with because of her busy family and travel schedule. Char retired in early 2013, a position which Ann would fill leading to our increased interaction. When Char retired, she thought she and her husband were going to move to Colorado or Washington. In the end they stayed right where they were, which after my move means that she lives some 10 minutes away. Lately, whenever I have dinner with Charlene we end up talking for two hours. Inevitably she will share something with me and say, "Now, I'm not telling everyone this." I take my role as confidante very seriously and with a sense of gratitude. My note to her read:

Charlene, a couple of years ago when you retired, you wrote me a thank you note which is still in my desk drawer. You ended your comments by saying "I look forward to years of friendship." I am so glad that we have remained friends and that we can continue to find adventures to share, whether they be in other states or simply other towns. I have always admired your grace, charm and ... what was the word? ... your agility. Tonight is about saying thank you to women that I admire and appreciate. Thank you for listening when I have needed a confidante. Thank you for cheerleading for me on Facebook. Thank you for continuing to nurture our friendship. And I too look forward to many more years of friendship, no matter where you and Bob land.

Of all the women listed here, **Linda** and I have been friends the longest. My friends have become her friends and her friends mine. She and I are great travel buddies because we both "never pass up a good bathroom." She was a bridesmaid at my wedding in 2008 and consoled me before, during and after my divorce. And that is Linda, a good friend through thick and thin. She has her own family of origin issues, so we get along great. My note to her read:

Linda, I have often told people that the one thing I always admired about my friend Grandma Jane was that anytime I invited her to do something she always had one of two responses ... "Sure, let's go!" OR "Sorry, I already have plans." She also was a great listener, because no matter what mood I was in she agreed with me. If I hated men, she knew enough bad guys that she understood. If I was in love, she had experienced love and understood that too. While Jane was a few decades older, I have always appreciated this same spirit in you. I firmly believe that we should surround ourselves with people who are honest enough to tell us the truth and biased enough to love us anyway. And that, my friend, is why I love you dearly.

I know this is a chapter about ladies who have a special place in my heart and life, but I need to add a quick note about two guys here. I would be remiss if I didn't mention them.

Nick is a former boss of mine. Years and years ago I began working for him as a temporary employee. I started on his birthday. I have told him since that I am the best present he ever got. We talk annually on our "anniversary." About three months after I started working for Nick, now a regular and full-time employee, he came into the office one morning looking horrible. It was obvious something was wrong. Nick asked me to come into his office where I would remain for a couple of hours. He opened his heart and soul to me and shared a great burden he was carrying. Why? In his words, "I just need to talk to someone and I sense that you are a good, Christian woman." I did what I could to help him through that time. About a year later, I was going through my first divorce. Nick and his wife Bonnie helped me in ways that I won't list here, partly because words would not do justice. Some 18 years later, Gracie wanted to take a gap year after high school and move to Philadelphia. I allowed her to do so in large part because Nick and Bonnie now lived there. If she needed help, I knew I would have trusted friends nearby who would readily step in. Nick and Bonnie are the kind of people who take "there for ya'" to a whole new level.

The other guy I need to mention is **Steve**, Linda's husband. By trade, Steve is a master mechanic. His garage is bigger than some houses with every tool and toy you can imagine. Steve is the kind of friend who is always there, no matter what. At one point I was looking to buy a different car. Steve and Linda came along so that Steve could check out the car before purchase. Not only did he help me find a good, used car; he negotiated the final sale price for me. In fact, at one point I think the salesman was tempted to just give me the car so he could avoid Steve's further beat down on the price. That's just who Steve is, always going the extra mile. Steve and I don't agree on politics and a few other matters. I was invited to speak at his 60th birthday party where we all had fun roasting him. I did so wearing a t-shirt promoting the political party which does not have Steve's support. This garnered much laughter from those gathered. Steve has my upmost respect and sincere gratitude for years of friendship. Now, if he would just quit pouting about the trip Linda and I took to New Orleans without him – three years ago, we'd be just fine.

These are the members of my chosen family. I can't imagine my life without them. I have no idea where I would be without their support. In reading this, I encourage you to give thanks for the people who have enriched your life in a special way. Reach out with a word of gratitude. And find ways to enrich the lives of others.

PS: Just before I was beginning to write this chapter, I was trying to decide how to organize it. My Facebook messenger went off and it was Karen, my Evil Twin. She sent me a picture … of the card that I had given her at the GNO. Totally out of the blue. No additional commentary. Just a single red heart in the corner of the screen that she had drawn. I asked her what made her send it then. She replied "I am going through a bunch of cards and found it because I wanted to save it. And WILL save it." It had not even dawned on me to use the text from those cards in this chapter. And that is absolutely the truth. It was another orchestrated "stars aligning" moment that I needed to help me finish this book.

Thanks, Twin, for the assistance. Mom (aka Tammy) still loves me more. And I am still the youngest.

Chapter 10 Reflection

"Finally, brethren, whatever things are true, whatever things are noble, whatever things are just, whatever things are pure, whatever things are lovely, whatever things are of good report, if there is any virtue and if there is anything praiseworthy – meditate on these things." Philippians 4:8

Q1: If you had to publicly acknowledge members of your own community of support, who would you include? Think of it as your Academy Award speech. You have 90 seconds to thank as many people as you can. Ready? Set? Go …

Q2: Each chapter in this book began with an emphasis word. Those were: Intentional, Hospitable, Transparent, Supportive, Compassionate, Aware, Social, Accepting, Motivated, and Grateful. Select two or three of those words and describe your own understanding of what it means or takes to build community with others. What other words would you add to your definition?

Q3: How has this book inspired you to build community with others?

Space intentionally left blank for your own thoughts.

Epilogue – A Seed Is Planted

I humbly consider this book to be part of God's eighth day of creation – only because it feels like all the stars have aligned for this to come to fruition. The line "I bow in humble adoration" came to mind as I finished drafting the chapter titled *Spreading Sonshine*. In fact, I asked Alexa to play the gospel song *How Great Thou Art* as I wrote the notes for this chapter, with three chapters left to write. I listened to it several times in an act of praise.

The seed for this book was planted years ago as I coached a recreational soccer team, something I had a blast doing. One of the players was nicknamed Pickle (real name Renee). Several years later, her mom, Kim, reached out to me on Facebook with an invitation to a local open mic storytelling event. "I think you'd like this," she simply said. SEED WAS PLANTED IN THE GROUND.

The first night I was at Story Slam I simply watched. The hostess, Shelly, used the line "This is all about building community." Over the months to come I began to agree. A DROP OF WATER FELL ONTO THE SEED.

As I participated with my own monthly stories, I began to get positive feedback from the audiences and my rotating band of personal groupies who came to support me. In essence, they were saying "Your story touched me" or that they found value in what I was saying. I found a place where I belonged. THE SEED BEGAN TO BREAK THROUGH THE SOIL.

In November, I shared my story briefly in church about giving a child up for adoption – unplanned and unrehearsed. This had two immediate effects on me. One, it spoke to the lady whose name I do not know who touched my arm and thanked me. Second, it impacted me profoundly for weeks as I pondered the notion that maybe what I had to say was important. It was to the point where I was asking friends to help me work through what was happening. I needed their perspective and support. As we talked, I simply asked them to keep me in their prayers as this all played out. PLANT IS NOW VISIBLE AND GROWING.

Within a span of 10 days in early January I had a series of events occur that throttled me forward ... the conversation with Myrna when she said, "I think I need to tell you to write a book"; the night when I was awakened with the vision outlining the chapters in the book; and the Martin Luther King, Jr. weekend when it snowed such that I was homebound and was afforded the time and quiet needed to write. FIRST BUDS BEGIN TO APPEAR ON THE PLANT.

Monday morning, with five chapters written and five more to go, I told Ann and Gracie about my project. Later in the day I told KJ. Over the coming weeks I would tell others. All were highly supportive. GARDENERS WERE HIRED TO HELP ME CARE FOR THE CREATION WITH WHICH I WAS BEING TRUSTED.

After I drafted the book, I sought guidance from Betsy. Her best advice to me was to walk away from my first draft and not edit it right away. I needed to allow some time so I could come back with fresh eyes and perspective. PREPARATION WAS MADE FOR HARVEST.

Months of continued inspiration and editing followed, with several readers involved. The chapter *Recycle Bin* was added mid-March. Friends shared my excitement as the time came closer to publish, fulfilling a long-standing dream of mine. I am an author who is very grateful for her community of support and for the inspiration which I have received.

With that, I encourage you to build community with those around you. Keep it simple. Be intentional, transparent, supportive and aware. Show compassion. Whether you extend hospitality to others, or experience the same in a social setting, be grateful for the people who accept you as you are. Admit your limitations and your challenges. Above all, I hope you are inspired by the stories shared here and that in telling your own stories you, too, can experience a rich sense of community. Let's keep the conversation going.

Acknowledgments

This book was literally spoken into being, prayed into being, and encouraged into being. In short, it took a community of people supporting me throughout the entire process to get my first book into your hands.

To Myrna, who on a cold, dreary January night in the midst of her extreme grief and sadness spoke this book into being. You have your dreams and I have mine. And we have at least two people looking down from heaven cheering us on.

To Dar, who patiently and faithfully prayed over every single word in this book multiple times as she read it and re-read it during the editing process. I doubt you knew what you were getting into when you sat on my couch in early February and I first asked you to be a part of this project. I have thanked you privately; I have thanked you publicly; but I doubt I can ever thank you enough.

To Jackie, Allyson, and Jane, my diligent editors. To Lisa and Peg who grilled me with questions regarding the purpose for this book and helped me refine the focus. To Paula who served as a sounding board on many occasions, and to John for his technical expertise.

To every single person who, upon first hearing that I was working on this book, said "Oh, I can't wait to read it!" The mere fact that you had the confidence that anything I wrote would be worth reading spoke volumes. I used your encouragement as sustenance to feed this dream. To my entire community of support … Thank you.

About the Author

Sandra j. Combs lives in Dayton, Ohio. She has a Bachelor of Arts from Oklahoma City University and a Master of Arts in Religious Communications from United Theological Seminary. She has worked in religious publishing as an editor, assistant editor, project manager, copy editor and writer. She has over 20 years of experience in corporate America as an Office Manager and Executive Assistant. Those are the things on her resume.

Let's face it, unless you flipped to the back of the book before reading it, you already know quite a bit about her from the stories told within. To make this interesting, here are a few random, fun facts about this first-time book author.

Sandra watches very little television. She would be happy with two channels on her TV – ESPN and The FoodNetwork.

She is an avid sports fan and can talk the talk on almost any sport, with the possible exception of rugby. If her athletic ability matched her competitive nature, she could have been an Olympian. Such was not the case.

If Sandra could meet any movie star, hands down it would be Tom Hanks. And in the movie of her life, Sandra Bullock will play the lead which of course makes sense – Sandra playing Sandra.

On Sandra's tombstone it will read "A recipient of Amazing Grace." Because she is.

Book #2, titled *God Moments*, is outlined. Stay tuned.